D0809166

The Critical Idiom
Founder Editor: John D. Jump (1969–1976)

43 Tragicomedy

Tragicomedy

David L. Hirst

Methuen
London and New York

First published in 1984 by
Methuen & Co. Ltd
11 New Fetter Lane,
London EC4P 4EE

Published in the USA by
Methuen & Co.
in association with Methuen, Inc.
733 Third Avenue,
New York, NY 10017

Typeset by
Scarborough Typesetting Services
and printed in Great Britain by
J. W. Arrowsmith (Bristol) Ltd

British Library
Cataloguing in Publication Data

Hirst, David Lawrence
  Tragicomedy.—
  (The Critical idiom;
  43)
  1. Tragicomedy
  I. Title.   II. Series
  809.2'512   PN1902

  ISBN 0–416–32760–5
  ISBN 0–416–32770–2 Pbk

Library of Congress
Cataloging in Publication Data

Hirst, David L.
  Tragicomedy.
  (The Critical idiom; 43)
  Bibliography: p.
  Includes index.
  1. Tragicomedy.   I. Title.
  PN1902.H57   1984
  809.2'523   84–671

  ISBN 0–416–32760–5
  ISBN 0–416–32770–2 (pbk.)

For Arnold in gratitude

Contents

Acknowledgements

I would like to thank the Italian Cultural Institute and in particular Dottore Ennio Troili for so generously enabling me to study in Italy. I am very grateful to Antony J. Simlick for typing the manuscript.

Preface

Tragicomedy has established itself in the twentieth century as the dominant dramatic form. The tragic hero no longer has the stature of Sophocles' Oedipus or Shakespeare's Lear: the modern Everyman is a figure like Arthur Miller's failed salesman Willy Loman, or Eugène Ionesco's absurd Bérenger; we accept as the theatrical norm such genres as black comedy, comedy of menace and savage farce; we evaluate the didactic potential of serious political drama from Edward Bond to Dario Fo in relation to the power of its humour. The further back we travel in dramatic history the easier it is to draw clear distinctions between tragedy and comedy; yet the two have always been complementary aspects of the impulse which creates theatre. Tragedy plays on our emotions, it involves us and demands our sympathy for the protagonist; comedy appeals to our intellect, we observe critically and laugh at the victim. Yet comedy may be considered the more serious of the two because it has a greater power to disturb the audience's conventional attitudes, whereas tragedy – certainly as justified by Aristotle – purifies, leaving us, in Milton's phrase, 'calm of mind, all passion spent'.

In choosing to combine these two dramatic forms a playwright has a crucial choice of method and aim: he can either employ a process of selection which leads to a careful synthesis of elements from the contrasted genres, or – conversely – he can create a volatile mix of tragedy and comedy so that different effects are contrasted. In the first case he will produce a play like *The Tempest* which, though titillating its audience with the potential of tragedy, spares them the harrowing experience of catharsis and leaves them relaxed and content. In the second case he will produce a play like *The Jew of Malta* which deliberately undermines the audience's feelings, denying them the involvement conducive to a sympathetic response and a consequent purgation of the feelings through pity and terror. In the former variety of tragicomedy the emotions are carefully tempered; in the latter they are stirred up and set against one another.

The neo-classical critics and dramatists of the Renaissance were the first to attempt to come to terms with the mixed genre. In England Sir Philip Sidney dismissed this 'mongrel' dramatic form as unworthy of consideration, while his Italian contemporary Giambattista Guarini wrote both a treatise and a drama in defence of it. Guarini's theory and practice are an important and useful landmark in the confusing expanse of plays which combine tragedy and comedy, since his guidelines help us to fix and evaluate those plays which fall within the category of tragicomedies seeking to effect a synthesis of contrasting elements. Guarini had a direct influence on writers of pastoral tragicomedy in England, notably on Beaumont and Fletcher and, through the latter, on Shakespeare. The plays of Corneille have a parallel method and aim. English melodrama of the nineteenth century, with its essentially escapist nature and palliative effect, employs a markedly similar formula to that utilized by Beaumont and Fletcher; it is carried over into the drama of two highly influential writers at the turn of the century: Shaw and Chekhov.

Guarini's theory cannot be applied to all plays in the mixed genre. As a result of the disintegration of confident distinctions between contrasted theatrical forms during the present century, his thesis has little relevance for the vast range of modern tragicomedies. Nor does it help towards an understanding of those plays which form the second branch of our study: those which seek to exploit a volatile mixture of contents. This tradition has had to wait until the twentieth century for any clear-cut definition: it is found in the works of Brecht and Artaud who, though they were not expressly writing tragicomedies, utilized sharp contrasts of mood and form in order to get away from a predominantly naturalistic theatre. Both Brecht's theory of Epic Theatre and Artaud's concept of a Theatre of Cruelty are a challenge to the more complacent implications of Aristotelian drama. And these two pioneers have precursors in the English medieval playwrights as well as in the dramatic satirists of the Elizabethan and Jacobean stage, while being in their turn the two most influential theorists and practitioners of the modern theatre.

In dealing with a theatrical genre so bewilderingly comprehensive and so long established, it is important to have certain central points of reference. The present study concentrates on two different but related areas. The first part compares neo-classical romance and satire, seeing the plays of Shakespeare, Fletcher and Corneille in the context of the literary theory of Guarini and contrasting them with the drama of Marlowe and the writers of revenge tragedy. The second part goes on to examine the parallel conflict of romanticism and realism in the nineteenth and twentieth centuries. We shall see that Chekhov and Shaw, influenced by the dominant popular idioms of melodrama, discovered fresh theatrical structures which have influenced the development of drama in the latter half of the twentieth century. The consideration of modern tragicomedy in the light of the theories of Brecht, Artaud and Pirandello provides us with a useful focus which complements the examination of sixteenth- and seventeenth-century theatre in relation to Renaissance concepts of stylistic propriety and dramatic form.

PART I

The sixteenth and seventeenth centuries: neo-classical romance and satire

1
Introduction

> *Mercury.* What's that? Are you disappointed
> To find it's a tragedy? Well, I can easily change it.
> I'm a god after all. I can easily make it a comedy,
> And never alter a line. Is that what you'd like? . . .
> But I was forgetting – stupid of me – of course,
> Being a god, I know quite well what you'd like.
> I know exactly what's in your minds. Very well.
> I'll meet you half way, and make it a *tragicomedy*.
>
> (Plautus, *Amphitryo*)

Giambattista Guarini's essay, *Compendio della Poesia Tragicomica*, published in 1601, was the first and remains the most substantial analysis of the tragicomic form. Written in late Renaissance Italy, it represents a justification of that mixed genre which was brought to its height at the turn of the sixteenth century. It has, on the one hand, the thoroughness and the significance of Aristotle's justification of tragedy in the *Poetics* and, on the other, the detailed examination of the implications of comedy we find in Meredith's celebrated essay *On Comedy* or Bergson's *Laughter*. Moreover, the *Compendio della Poesia Tragicomica* is closely related to Guarini's drama *Il Pastor Fido* which triumphantly reveals the author's theories in practice. Key works of the neo-classical school, the essay and the play both point back to the origins of drama in fifth-century BC Athens while foreshadowing the tragicomedy of the early Jacobean period in England and the mid-seventeenth century in France. Both of Guarini's influential writings were pioneer works; thanks to him tragicomedy established itself as a valid new genre. But just as his own theories came out of his practice – not vice versa – so future playwrights were to explore and extend this dramatic form as well as the implications of his critique.

Guarini's *Compendio* – so termed because it is an amalgamation of two related studies – is concerned to counter the two basic Renaissance arguments against tragicomedy: that it is a mixed form combining tragedy and comedy; and that it lacks unity of action as it grafts one subject on another. He defends the mixed form, making analogies with the hermaphrodite and with the alloy, bronze, before employing the example of the doctor who employs a substance extracted from the venom of the snake itself as an antidote for snake bite. The point is that this substance has been tempered: only what is beneficial has been utilized. This, he goes on to argue, is what the writer of tragicomedy should do: take what he needs from the contrasted genres of tragedy and comedy. From the former he takes 'noble characters not noble actions, a story which is credible but not historically true, heightened yet tempered effects, delight not sorrow, the danger not the death', and from the latter 'laughter which is not dissolute, modest pleasures, a feigned crisis, an unexpected happy ending and – above all – the comic plotting' (*Compendio*, p. 231). This requires a fuller explanation. From tragedy Guarini takes public figures but private actions. It is clear from his distinction earlier in the essay between the tragic hero – 'la persona grande' – and the proper subjects of comedy – 'persona e negozio privato' (i.e. the ordinary man and his affairs) – that he is demanding a fusion of the fundamental and contrasted bases of the two genres. He requires a believable but not a true story: again tragedy traditionally dealt with epic heroes, comedy with invented characters or (as in the case of Aristophanes) with contemporaries. Guarini wishes the emotions to be heightened, but tempered (the key word, as in the analogy with snake bite, is 'rintuzzati'). The audience is to experience the aesthetic pleasure of participating without the full emotional consequences brought about by a tragic catharsis. This is achieved by threatening the characters with danger but not allowing any of them actually to die. The first four characteristics he takes from comedy are relatively straightforward: laughter that is not bawdy (while it is in the plays of Aristophanes or Plautus),

less emotionally demanding drama, apparent threats to the characters, and a surprise dénouement. What is more complex – and, as
he says here, most important, an issue to which he returns in detail
later – is the 'ordine comico'. This is the detailed comic plotting:
the development and working out of intrigues which, in their
intricacy, are the province of comedy and not of tragedy.

He tackles the subject of unity of action later in the essay when
he compares tragicomedy to different types of tragedy. As against
the tragedy with one plot and one outcome are two others: the
mixed type with two issues and the tragedy with a happy ending.
In the first category could be included Sophocles' *Electra*, in the
second Euripides' *Orestes*. Cunningly, after suggesting that Aristotle considers and allows all three, albeit preferring the first, he
goes on to argue the superiority of tragicomedy over both the
cruder precursors of the mixed genre in that it has one basic
intrigue, one denouement and a happy ending which involves all
the characters. Earlier in the essay he casts doubt on the validity of
Aristotle's theory of catharsis by asking such pointed questions as:
'How can we be purged of pity without at the same time being
stripped of all humanity?' and 'How can it be that terrible events
purge fear?' (p. 235). These questions anticipate his own theory as
to how tragicomedy should work. He draws an important distinction between the 'technical' ('strumentale') and the 'overall'
('architettonico') objectives of drama. Aristotle's definition of
tragedy – that its technical and overall ends are respectively the
imitation of horrifying and pitiful events and the purgation of the
pity and fear they arouse – is complemented by a parallel theory of
Guarini's on comedy. He suggests that its technical aim is the
imitation of the actions of private men whose mistakes move us to
laughter, while its overall objective is the purgation of melancholy
in order to gladden our soul. This culminates in the complex but
logical formulation that the aim of tragicomedy is therefore:

> to imitate through the *mise en scène* a contrived action which
> combines all the tragic and comic elements which can believably

and decorously coexist, regulated within the framework of a
unified dramatic form whose aim is to purge with delight the
sadness of the audience. In such a way that Imitation – the
'technical' objective – is a mixed one, because it represents a
combination of tragic and comic elements. Whereas Purgation
– the 'overall' objective – is a single one because it reduces this
combination of elements to one basic concept: the liberation of
the audience from melancholy.

                                                    (*Compendio*, p. 246)

Guarini was writing at a watershed in dramatic history. In
attempting to justify his own theatrical work he was imposing a
system, clarifying the inconsistencies in the writing of his immediate precursors, men like Giraldi Cinthio who in his plays and
his theoretical writings – most notably the *Discourse on Comedy
and Tragedy* published in 1556 – had envisaged a more complex
relationship between these dramatic forms than that outlined by
Aristotle. Taking Guarini's thesis as a focal point, we may usefully
glance back to the origins of drama and forward to the theatre of
our own times in order to place his theory in the context of the
development of this complex genre. Guarini's pronounced criticism of Aristotle sought to elucidate some of the contradictions he
felt were implicit in the *Poetics*. It is much easier to formulate a
theory of tragedy than one of comedy (as the contrasted work of
Aristotle, Bergson and Meredith in these fields reveals); it is even
more difficult – particularly at this point in time – to pin down
precisely the tragicomic form. Aristotle encountered difficulties
when he was forced to deal with those plays which are not straightforwardly tragic. He is crystal clear and illuminating in his comments on Sophocles' *Oedipus Rex*; but not every tragedy – even in
fifth-century BC Athens – conforms to the ideal model which he
praised here. Sophocles' sequel *Oedipus at Colonus* is constructed
in a wholly different way, dealing as it does with the hero's enlightenment. This should alert us to consider the dramas – as Aristotle
did not – within the context of the trilogy which formed the basis

of each day's entertainment during the Dionysia. Similarly *The Eumenides*, the final play in the sole extant trilogy, Aeschylus' *Oresteia*, at the end converts vengeance to pity: a comic, or rather, tragicomic outcome.

If Sophocles' *Electra* provided an example of what Guarini calls a 'tragedy with a double outcome' in that the wicked (Clytemnestra and Aegisthus) are punished while the good (Electra and Orestes) triumph, how much more difficult to classify is Euripides' sequel, *Orestes*, in which the issue of justice, treated in the abstract by Aeschylus, is here brought down to a personal family level as Orestes and Electra set themselves against Menelaus, Helen and Hermione? Most problematic is the ending in which Apollo intervenes, announcing that Helen has been saved and that the opposing factions should make their peace and seal it with Orestes' marriage to the woman whose life he has just threatened. It is precisely because Euripides challenged the traditional heroic values that he moved into the realm of satire and in so doing attacked the whole basis of tragedy, thus preparing the way for a mixed genre when drama was revived in the neo-classical period. Few of his plays are tragic in any Aristotelian sense, even *The Trojan Women* being wholly different in structure from the model outlined in the *Poetics*. If the more epic structure of *The Phoenician Women* is matched by the savage ironies of *The Bacchae*, a play like *Iphigenia in Tauris* is nearer romance than tragedy. It averts a threatened death in the happy reconciliation of brother and sister and employs the tragic effects of reversal (peripeteia) and recognition (*anagnorisis*) for purposes closer to comedy. It remains significant, however, that Euripides is begging questions within the firm framework of tragedy. Nowhere does he introduce characters from an alien genre nor employ devices – of plotting and intrigue – peculiar to comedy. Nor are his plays, indeed, funny; the ironies point up human frailty in contrasting the ideal with the real; they are not intended to provoke laughter.

Comedy in both classical Greece and Rome was a dramatic form totally independent of tragedy. The plays of Aristophanes are bawdy, their stories inventions, their characters often taken from contemporary Athenian life. Polonius was later to remark, of the players in *Hamlet*: 'Seneca cannot be too heavy nor Plautus too light' (II. ii. 396–7). In employing characters from a different world – citizens and their slaves – Roman comedy had nothing in common with tragedy which, as exemplified in the plays of Seneca, handled the familiar Greek stories, adapting them to the tastes of Nero and his court. Plautus' *Amphitryo*, frequently cited in the neo-classical period as the exception, represents no more than the exception which proves the rule. It is an exception only in that it mixes gods with noble characters and comic servants, but since the two gods behave entirely as the coarsest of mortals (which is the comic point) the play is remarkable only because it asks us to believe that Jupiter and Alcmene are having a passionate affair although she is nine months' pregnant. A far more influential play – at least in determining the form of *Il Pastor Fido* – is Terence's *Andria* which Guarini praised for the interdependence of separate strands of the plot, and which, though a pure comedy, was to provide him with the situation – equally productive in his drama of tragic and comic potential – in which the arbitrary decision of parents to marry off their children is averted by the revelation of the true parentage of another child.

It is important to define precisely what tragicomedy implies and this can be done not so much through a fixed definition as through an assessment of how a tradition has developed and to what extent the blueprint evolved by Guarini has been utilized and adapted by succeeding dramatists. While Guarini was working on *Il Pastor Fido*, Sir Philip Sidney had something very different to say about tragicomedy. In *The Defence of Poesie* (1583) he is heavily dismissive of drama as a whole, arguing:

> But beside these gross absurdities, how all their plays be neither right tragedies nor right comedies, mingling kings and clowns, not because the matter so carrieth it but thrust in the clown by head and shoulders to play a part in majestical matters, with

neither decency nor discretion; so as neither the admiration and commiseration, nor the right sportfulness is by their mongrel tragicomedy obtained. I know Apuleius did somewhat so, but that is a thing recounted with space of time, not represented in one moment; and I know the ancients have one or two examples of tragicomedies, as Plautus hath *Amphitryo*. But if we mark them well we shall find that they never, or very daintily match hornpipes and funerals.

(p. 67)

When Sidney was writing this, Burbage's theatre, the first professional English playhouse, had only been in existence for seven years. It is impossible to know quite what Sidney would have thought of the performances then at the beginning of the new century, if he had lived to see them, but his analysis of contemporary theatre was accurate. The very strengths which were to give the new dramatic movement such force – the ability to represent every facet of human activity and to utilize a wide variety of dramatic techniques – were inherent in the jumbled hotchpotch of theatrical effects which were already being clumsily thrown together in contemporary stage works.

We can see why Sidney was so harsh if we glance at a play like Thomas Preston's *Cambises* which marks a fascinating transition between the medieval drama and the new theatre which was to flourish at the end of the century. It is described in the frontispiece as:

A lamentable tragedy mixed full of pleasant mirth containing the life of Cambises, King of Persia from the beginning of his kingdom unto his death, his one good deed of execution, after that many wicked deeds and tyrannous murders committed by and through him, and last of all his odious death by gods justice appointed.

The play was obviously popular: Falstaff reproves Hal in *King Henry IV, Part 1* with the words: 'for I must speak in passion, and

I will do it in King Cambises' vein' (II. iv. 381–2), while its structure (and title) are parodied in *A Midsummer Night's Dream* whose
play-within-a-play is called 'A tedious brief scene of young
Pyramus / And his love Thisbe, very tragical mirth' (V. i. 56–7).
Cambises is an Interlude, taking features from the medieval Moralities and the Miracle tradition, but developing them into a political
history play which attempts tragedy and also incorporates scenes
of low-life comedy. Polonius would have had great difficulty in
finding the right genre from among his 'tragedy, comedy, history,
pastoral, pastoral-comical, historical-pastoral, tragical-historical,
tragical-comical-historical-pastoral' (II. ii. 392–5) – itself a comment on the fatuousness of attempting to categorize English drama
of this period. *Cambises* concerns a tyrannical monarch who after
perpetrating several murders is himself killed in a riding accident.
The transitional stage between Morality and Tudor history play is
seen in the mingling of abstractions such as Common's Complaint
and Small Ability with historical figures, while the involvement of
comic characters such as Huf, Snuf and Ruf or the prostitute
Meretrix, anticipates Shakespeare's technique in the second historical tetralogy. Such a play broke every rule of Aristotelian stage-
craft: it indiscriminately combines characters and techniques
appropriate to wholly different dramatic forms; nor does it in any
way relate to Guarini's careful amalgamation of the genres.

The most interesting – and for our purposes the most significant
– character in the play, however, is the Vice, Ambidexter, who
tempts and thus manipulates many of the figures from the judge,
Sisamnes, down to the comic characters, Hob and Lob. The stage
directions for his first appearance read: 'Enter the Vice with an
olde capcase on his hed, an olde pail about his hips for harnes, a
scummer and a potlid by his side, and a rake on his shoulder'; he
soon makes his presence felt:

> My name is Ambidexter. I signifie one
> That with bothe handes finely can play,
> Now with king Cambises and by and by gone.

Thus doo I run this way and that way.
For (a) while I meane with a souldier to be,
Then give I a leape to Sisamnes the judge.
I dare avouch you shall his destruction see.
To all kinde of estates I meane for to trudge.

(Cambises, 149–56)

This figure, in part the devil, in part the stage fool, is a personification of the Dionysiac drive in English drama. He is also, as far as
the English theatre is concerned, a personification of the tragicomic spirit: a creation far removed from the neo-classical world of
Guarini. A forerunner of Ambidexter is Mak, the Sheepstealer in
the Towneley *Second Shepherd's Play*, also a diabolic as well as a
comic figure. He will take different shapes as the native drama
becomes more sophisticated: the Jew of Malta, Richard III and a
whole string of clowns in Shakespeare, most notably Lucio, Lear's
Fool and Caliban. All these characters are highly unpredictable:
like the joker in a pack of cards they are capable of affecting profoundly the relationship between the other characters. The figure
reappears as the malcontent in so many later revenge plays, highlighting the tragicomic nature of so much Elizabethan and Jacobean drama in which tragedy is shot through with comedy, either
in flashes (as in the plays of Webster), or in a whole series of carefully contrasted scenes (as in Marlowe) or as a means of complicat-
ing the audience's emotional response (as in Shakespeare).

This tradition has nothing in common with the classical inheritance exemplified in the work of Guarini, but it is a powerful fusion
of contrasted genres with an ancestry in medieval drama which it
would be foolish to ignore. In adapting biblical stories the medieval
dramatists in England were attempting to provide plays which –
like those in classical Greece – represented an enactment of myth
for a festive occasion. Though the material was Christian many of
the methods of presentation were pagan, as the Church was quick to
see and exploit. As drama emerged in England it differed radically
from that evolved in Greece by virtue of the cyclical presentation

which encouraged a juxtaposition of opposites – pathos, laughter, piety, bawdy. Biblical stories yielded drama which inclined alternately towards tragedy, comedy and satire (political and social), thus revealing in embryo all the genres that were to be developed – and often fused – in the Elizabethan period. The most fundamental narratives – the fall of man, the flood, the crucifixion – are quite differently handled in different cycles, so that in the York story of Adam and Eve the Vice makes his first appearance as a partly comic Satan; the Chester and Wakefield cycles make – very contrasted – comedies of the Noah story; while the crucifixion is a subject for pointed realistic humour at York and for grim, psychologically disturbing satire at Wakefield. Several of the characters invented by the Wakefield 'Master' – Pikeharness (in the *Killing of Abel*), Froward (in the *Buffetting*) – have affinities with Mak: they are dangerous clowns.

It was this richness of material which Sidney deplored and which, when developed fully in the professional theatre, was to set English Renaissance drama in the forefront of world theatre. Dramatists at the end of the sixteenth century discovered a vital new medium which was infinite in potential. They did not follow classical precedent or academic rules; they adapted forms to present their material and in so doing broke down all the neatly defined categories.

The drama of this period evades any such classification as is provided by either Guarini or Aristotle, but at one specific point, the end of the first decade of the seventeenth century, England was clearly taking note of Guarini. In 1608 Fletcher produced a play called *The Faithful Shepherdess* which is indebted to Guarini's theory and practice. Echoing the definition of pastoral in the *Compendio*, Fletcher emphasizes in his preface: 'you are ever to remember shepherds to be such as all the ancient poets, and modern, of understanding, have received them: that is the owners of flocks and not Hirelings' (p. 14). He goes on to discuss dramatic form with reference to some of the basic points of Guarini's essay:

A tragicomedy is not so called in respect of mirth and killing, but in respect it wants deaths, which is enough to make it no tragedy, yet brings some near it, which is enough to make it no comedy, which must be a representation of familiar people, with such kind of trouble as no life be questioned; so that a god is as lawful in this as in a tragedy, and mean people as in a comedy.

(p. 14)

Fletcher was here adapting Guarini's thesis to the specific ends of English drama: the first part of the above quotation is a version of Guarini's 'Il pericolo non la morte'; the second, however, has a native emphasis, unlike Guarini's 'le persone grandi, non l'azione'. The drama of Beaumont and Fletcher, as well as the plays of Shakespeare after his company moved to the Blackfriars Theatre towards the end of his career in 1608, show an attempt to explore romance – often pastoral romance – and to give unity and dramatic cogency to this genre. The finest example of this new dramatic form is *The Tempest* which explores fundamental Shakespearian themes with a freshness and force resulting from a discipline akin to that advocated by Guarini.

The flowering of tragicomedy in the Guarini mould was short-lived in England. We must move to France in the middle of the seventeenth century to see the implications of his neo-classical theories pushed further. The plays of Pierre Corneille in particular represent an important attempt to create a genuine 'third type', a fusion of tragedy and comedy such as Guarini envisaged in his analogies with the hermaphrodite who is a true mixture and female, or bronze which is an alloy of copper and tin. Writing for a sophisticated audience, playwrights sought to evolve dramatic forms that were firm enough to organize and control the passionate, destructive emotions and yet sufficiently flexible to express through restraint every nuance of feeling. Racine's tragedies and Molière's comedies represent contrasted expressions of this same ethic; tragicomedy is a more complex achievement than either. The political and social instability of England during this period, plus the closure of theatres during the Puritan interregnum, meant that no comparable harmonizing of passion and intellect characterized the contemporary English stage. Indeed, when Dryden wrote his celebrated essay *Of Dramatick Poesie* in 1668 the new theatre was in its infancy. It is not surprising to find Dryden, through the four speakers who debate the issues, undecided as to the validity of tragicomedy. Lisideius echoes Sidney's sentiments when he says:

> there is no Theatre in the world has anything so absurd as the English Tragicomedie, 'tis a *Drama* of our own invention, and the fashion of it is enough to proclaim it so; here a course of mirth, there another of sadness and passion; and a third of honour and a Duel: Thus in two hours and a half, we run through all the fits of *Bedlam*.
>
> (*Of Dramatick Poesie*, p. 65)

Later Neander, taking up this point, may well be given the last word, challenging Lisideius's contention that 'mirth and compassion (are) things incompatible' with the point that 'contraries, when placed near set off each other'; but the latter argument lacks the bite and wit of the former and Neander's assertion is distinctly limp, essentially a chauvinistic appeal rather than an analysis of the issue in any depth:

> A scene of mirth, mix'd with Tragedy has the same effect upon us which our musick has betwixt the Acts, which we find a relief to us from the best Plots and language of the Stage, if the discourses have been long. I must therefore have stronger arguments, ere I am convinc'd, that compassion and mirth in the same subject destroy each other, and in the mean time cannot but conclude, to the honour of our Nation that we have invented, increas'd and perfected a more pleasant way for the Stage than was ever known to the Ancients or Moderns of any Nation, which is Tragicomedie.
>
> (pp. 77–8)

Dryden's plays reveal the influence of neo-classical ideas in England but the undoubted superiority of contemporary French tragedy and tragicomedy which related practice to a clear set of principles is highlighted by Dryden's handling of two Shakespearian dramas: his *All for Love* emasculates the story of Antony and Cleopatra by slavish observation of the unities of time, place and action; while his version (with Davenant) of *The Tempest* entirely disregards Shakespeare's careful observation of the unities and through spurious elaboration destroys the careful structuring of Shakespeare's last tragicomedy.

Dryden was right to champion the superiority of English drama in the early part of the seventeenth century, even if he did it for the wrong reasons. His essay was written before the Comedy of Manners established itself as the most vital theatrical form in the late seventeenth century. It is here – in the plays of Wycherley and Congreve most notably – that the English comic tradition continued most powerfully. Here that peculiarly English brand of tragicomedy again manifests itself, that volatile confrontation of opposites in a satiric mode which, though it does not embrace tragedy, is the least romantic genre of comedy. Though characters are not threatened with death, they are often ruined, both sexually and financially, and one needs only glance at Pinchwife's savage physical threats to his wife, the conduct of Olivia and Vernish in Wycherley's *The Plain Dealer*, or the machinations of villains like Maskwell and Fainall to realize the serious implications of this comic genre. In a sense it is the antithesis of tragicomedy which – from Guarini to Beckett – tends to avoid realism. The conduct of the rakes in the comedy of the post-Restoration period is both unscrupulous and down to earth. They are – in the persons of a Horner or a Dorimant – Don Juans, but their mode of conduct differs greatly from Molière's anti-hero. When Mozart and Da Ponte put the character on stage again in the eighteenth century, they did so in a work which is arguably one of the finest of tragicomedies, one which, though its protagonist is dragged off to hell, was described by its creator as a 'dramma giocosa'. It was Beaumarchais, whose play *The Marriage of Figaro* was also transformed by Mozart and Da Ponte into a far more complex blend of the humorous and the pathetic, not least through the agency of the music (often, as we shall see, an important constituent of tragicomedy) who made this challenging point in the *Lettre Modérée sur la Chute et la Critique du Barbier de Séville* (1775):

> An amorous old man intends to marry his ward on the morrow; a more skilful young rival intervenes and cocks a snook at the guardian by marrying her this very day in the guardian's own house. This is the basic material from which one could equally have fashioned a tragedy, a comedy, a melodrama or tragicomic drama, an opera, etc. What more is there to Molière's *L'Avare*? What more is there to *Le Grand Mithridate*? The genre of a play, like that of any activity, depends less on the basic material than on the characters which bring it to life.
>
> (ed. A. Dobson, Oxford, 1884, pp. 62–3)

'What more there is' to those dramas which we may term tragicomedies is precisely the topic of this study. Though 'basic material' may be adapted in a variety of ways, the resultant genre depends on much more than 'the characters who bring it to life': it depends on a careful construction or adaptation of dramatic form to guide and affect the audience's responses. It is through a consideration of form that we can most helpfully reach an evaluation and definition of those plays discussed in our survey, which inevitably covers a variety of theatrical genres.

By comparing (in Chapters 2 and 3 respectively) the Jacobean pastoral tragicomedies with the tragedies and revenge plays of the same period we can observe two quite different methods of carefully evolving a theatrical structure which combines pathos and humour. The tragicomedies of Corneille (discussed in Chapter 4) as against the bleaker comedies of Molière represent a further development of these contrasted approaches. Chapter 5 discusses those features of English nineteenth-century melodrama which have affinities with the plays analysed in Chapter 2; and the persistence of this formula is explored in the dramas of both Chekhov and Shaw which occupy Chapter 6. The penultimate chapter looks beyond the methods established by these two writers; it deals with the pioneer works of Pirandello, Artaud and Brecht in the inter-war period and the Theatre of the Absurd after the Second World War, all important attempts to find fresh and meaningful forms for exploring alternatives to tragedy. The final chapter, by examining a careful selection of contrasted modern writers in relation to the traditions and conventions discussed previously, lays down guidelines for a more informed appreciation of the contemporary theatrical scene which is characterized by the breakdown of established dramatic categories.

2
Seventeenth-century pastoral and tragicomedy

> *Coro.* Non è sana ogni gioia,
>   né mal cio che v'annoia.
>   Quello è vero gioire,
>   che nasce da virtù dopo il soffrire.
>   (Giambattista Guarini, *Il Pastor Fido*)

> *Chorus.*   All is not joy
>   That tickles us; nor is all that annoy
>   That goes down bitter. True joy is a thing
>   That springs from virtue after suffering.
>   (*The Faithful Shepherd*, trans. Richard Fanshawe)

The last part of Guarini's *Compendio* is concerned at length with *Il Pastor Fido*. Here the author explains in detail his formula for composing a tragicomedy, illustrating his theory by detailed reference to the play. The drama, which he began as early as 1569 and which was published in 1589, being first performed in Mantua in 1598 with much splendour and success, was still the subject of critical debate at the turn of the century when he published the *Compendio*. It is important, therefore, before we go on to discuss its influence on the related genres of pastoral and romance in Jacobean England, to look more precisely at the author's formulations. Guarini is as specific as Aristotle in his discussion of dramatic form. He emphasizes that in the first act the first thing which must be established in order that the audience may be clear about the plot and its development is the pressing or crucial issue ('urgente cagione') on which all the parts of the work are dependent. It is also vital from the start to establish the genre: hence the scenes must be carefully contrasted, the serious and tragic with the pleasant and comic. Act II must be concerned with intensifying the complexity of the plot, thereby sustaining the interest and delight of the audience by giving it something fresh on which to chew ('nuovo cibo'). Four conditions circumscribe this new material: it must consist not merely of words, but also deeds; it must not destroy the unity of action; it must help the developing intrigue; and it must not serve to give away the final outcome. Guarini has already employed a telling image – the enticements of the loose woman who offers 'baits to desire' – to explain the importance of keeping the audience constantly in suspense. In Act III the techniques of the previous act must be intensified by original and unlooked-for twists of plot. Here Guarini discusses the importance of the 'ordine comico', the comic plotting, which is very different from the more open, less devious plotting of tragedy. Comic intrigue, Guarini tells us, thrives on cunning, lying, deceit, shrewdness, trickery: far removed from the gravity of tragedy. Act IV is 'tutto nodo': the climax of the intrigue. Here – in contrast to the comic implications of the previous act – everyone is brought to the height of suffering: the 'danger' is most extreme, the threats of 'death' most intense. The last act concerns itself with the 'credible miracle' which is basic to the comic dénouement. Vital to this are three aspects: the way in which it is prepared (the groundwork, 'fondamento', has to be laid in the previous act); the discovery itself (which must be skilfully handled); and the joy and pleasure which are consequent on its outcome.

A brief description of the plot of *Il Pastor Fido* will illustrate precisely how Guarini achieves all this. In Act I we learn of Montano's plan to marry his son Silvio to Amarilli in the hope of fulfilling an ancient prophecy and thus ending the sufferings of Arcadia consequent upon the betrayal many years previously of the faithful shepherd, Aminta. Silvio, however, prefers hunting to women, while Amarilli is secretly loved by Mirtillo. However, Corisca is determined to seduce Mirtillo. This angers Satiro who, rejected by Corisca, plans revenge. (Guarini defines the five scenes of this act as being alternately: pleasant, serious, comic, tragic and wholly comic.) In Act II Corisca advances her plan by befriending the innocent Amarilli and offering to help her get rid of an unwanted husband; we are also introduced to Dorinda, who is hopelessly in love with Silvio, and her comic servant, a goatherd, Lupino. Act III is concerned with the details of Corisca's intrigue: after Mirtillo has been rebuked by Amarilli, Corisca eavesdrops on her confession (in the sort of soliloquy others can hear) that she actually loves Mirtillo. Corisca, telling her that Silvio's coldness is due to his love for Lisetta – a total invention – persuades her to catch the two together in a cave. She then tells Mirtillo that Amarilli has a secret rendezvous with another shepherd; when he sees Amarilli approaching the cave, Mirtillo, misinterpreting her asides, decides to follow her, catch her with her lover, kill them both and then himself. As he enters the cave his asides are in turn misinterpreted by Satiro who thinks he is meeting Corisca there and seals the mouth of the cave with a rock, then goes off to fetch the priests. In Act IV a sentence of death is passed on Amarilli for lechery and Corisca is triumphant. Meanwhile – and preparing us for the happy outcome of Act V – Silvio, congratulating himself on being free of the love which has brought Amarilli and Mirtillo to their present predicament, accidentally wounds Dorinda and is converted by her suffering to love her. A sequence of events following on the apparent catastrophe of the previous act turn the outcome into a happy one for all. The sacrifice of Mirtillo, who insists on dying for Amarilli, is interrupted by the arrival of Carino, his supposed father. In the revelations which follow Amarilli is proven innocent and it transpires that Mirtillo is the lost son of Montano: thus in their marriage the ancient prophecy can be fulfilled. Seeing the joy of the lovers, Corisca is repentant and begs their forgiveness.

Several points about the construction of the play deserves special mention. Guarini keeps us guessing right to the end; each twist of the plot comes as a surprise, yet is credible. Guarini claims that the test of how successfully the unity of action has been observed is whether or not you can extract any thread of the plot or any character without destroying the whole. With *Il Pastor Fido* you cannot. Moreover, though he does not discuss this, Guarini observes the unity of time (the action is continuous) and the unity of place (in that the scene is Arcadia). There are powerful consequences in the non-observation of these unities in the tragicomedies performed on the Jacobean stage. The three aspects of the dénouement are discussed by Guarini. He argues that we are prepared for the happy outcome by Mirtillo's character, the fortuitous arrival of Carino and the inexorable train of events which follows. The discovery is in two parts, brought about by a combination of techniques taken from *Oedipus Rex* and *Iphigenia in Tauris*, the author insisting on the superiority of a recognition through discussion rather than external signs. He also points out the importance of Corisca's repentance: if she were left unhappy, a mixed tragedy ('di doppia costituzione') would result; nor should she be allowed, as a wicked character, to succeed. The mixture of tragedy and comedy is also successfully effected, notably in Corisca's scheming in Act III in which her object (the threatened death of Amarilli) is tragic, but her way of going about it is entirely within the conventions of comedy. The threatened death of Amarilli in Act IV and of Mirtillo in Act V culminate in Montano's horror that he must kill his own son. Finally the situation is resolved by a blind old seer, Tirenio. Thus the tragic emotional appeal is first heightened and then tempered by the change of events.

In Fletcher's *The Faithful Shepherdess* Italian theory and practice first made themselves felt in England. Though in its effect and particularly in its overall objective, Fletcher's pastoral tragicomedy is very different from Guarini's, the young English dramatist, destined to be the bright hope of the King's Men after Shakespeare's retirement a few years later, had clearly read both *Il Pastor Fido* and the *Compendio*. This is most evident in the unity of the play. The various strands of the plot are inextricably tied together, the action is continuous and takes place in a wood in

Thessaly. Moreover the characters are all shepherds. Fletcher had clearly taken Guarini's point that:

> In *Il Pastor Fido*, therefore, there are not three stories, one with ordinary ('private') people who perform the comic action, another with public ('grandi') figures who enact the tragic part, and a third with shepherds who contribute the pastoral element: but one single story concerning pastoral figures which mingles tragedy and comedy, interwoven in the manner of comedy, and constituting a unified poem.

> (*Compendio*, p. 274)

In short this is not *The Winter's Tale*. Even though the details of his story are different and the comedy far more bawdy than Italian neo-classical taste would allow, Fletcher follows Guarini to a fault. As Philip Edwards puts it, '[the] principle of architectural wholeness which is so necessary to the romantic type of tragicomedy . . . is set forth in diagrammatic form, and in slow motion tempo in *The Faithful Shepherdess*' ('The danger not the death: the art of John Fletcher', Stratford-upon-Avon Studies, I, p. 174). But Edwards rightly points out that the theme of the work, the 'careful ranging of kinds of love and lust', owes less to Guarini than to the English pastoral writers Sidney and Spenser (and to Book III of *The Faerie Queene* in particular) whose concerns Fletcher (and later Beaumont with him) attempted to translate into theatrical terms for the court of James I. In pushing the lustful qualities of Guarini's Corisca very much to the fore, Fletcher reveals himself to be writing for a very different kind of audience from Guarini's. Fletcher's audience strongly anticipates that which reassembled after the Civil War and which, as we know from Dryden's high praise of Beaumont and Fletcher, would undoubtedly have relished such lines as Chloe's: 'It is impossible to ravish me / I am so willing' (*The Faithful Shepherdess*, II. i. 375).

Philaster (1608) – written by Beaumont and Fletcher in collaboration – bears every mark of having been composed to the Guarinian formula. The marriage of Arethusa to Pharamond, forced on her by her father, is the 'urgente cagione' which sets everything in motion. The first act, in contrasting scenes of political necessity, love and (bawdy) comedy, clearly establishes the mixed genre. Bellario's unwillingness to leave Philaster and Galatea's determination (after overhearing Pharamond's immodest proposal to Megra) 'to lay a train to blow [their] sports up' advances the action of Act II. In Act III the action is complicated further by Megra's accusation of Arethusa and Dion's further deceit, a 'subtle train' by which Bellario is 'abused'. The plotting of Act III – entirely in accord with Guarini's 'ordine comico' – gives way to the contrasted tragic mood of Act IV in which the central trio all suffer emotionally and are in turn wounded physically. In the last act the innocence of Bellario and Arethusa is proven, Philaster marries Arethusa, the King regrets his actions and the two villains – Megra and Pharamond – are banished. All the parts of the action are entirely interdependent, and the unities of time and place are not abused. It is when we come to consider the overall objective (Guarini's 'fine architettonico') that we become more aware of the hollowness of the play. Una Ellis-Fermor has defended the work of Beaumont and Fletcher as being valid in creating a particular mood, one which, she argues, can be applied just as successfully to comedy or tragedy as to tragicomedy. Speaking of Philaster's conversation with Bellario in Act III, scene i she writes:

> It is in scenes like these that the finest flowering of the tragicomedy romantic mood is to be found, working in its own proper medium and uncontaminated by incongruous association, moral or aesthetic, uncontaminated too by reference to that world of tragic doubt and horror or satiric exposure that was the Jacobean tragedy and comedy.
>
> (*The Jacobean Drama*, p. 220)

This smacks of special pleading. The playwrights are not, as she claims elsewhere in the essay, sacrificing dramatic structure for emotional effects; rather they are too slavishly following a formula.

They were undoubtedly opportunists exploiting the potential of a continental model, though it is not necessary to go quite as far as John Danby and see this as 'sinister': that they were 'unconsciously fighting a rearguard action on behalf of the court, compensating with advances in Blackfriars for the retreats in Westminster' ('Beaumont and Fletcher: Jacobean absolutists', *Elizabethan Drama*, p. 294). The derivative quality which Danby castigates in his analysis of their work, and of this play in particular, is attributable more to their imitation of *Il Pastor Fido* than Sir Philip Sidney's pastoral *Arcadia*.

A few years later Fletcher was writing plays – in collaboration with Beaumont, Massinger and Shakespeare – which, in extending the implications of tragicomedy in England, got well out of the shadow of Guarini. One thing Fletcher had certainly taken to heart was Guarini's insistence that the playwright tease the audience to the last minute by giving just enough and not too much away – a strategy particularly appropriate to tragicomedy with its surprising reversal of fortunes from bad to good. In a poem prefacing the First Folio, the Stuart poet and dramatist William Cartwright praised this quality in the plays:

> None can prevent the fancy, and see through
> At the first opening; all stand wondering how
> The thing will be, until it is; which hence
> With fresh delight still cheats, still takes the sense;
> The whole design, the shadow, the lights such
> That none can say he shews or hides too much.

This is a technique akin to that of the writer of detective fiction, and the pleasure it gives is sufficient in itself. It is futile to search for a deeper, more serious purpose when this becomes the *sine qua non* of the play, as it does, for example in Beaumont and Fletcher's *A King and No King* (1611). The 'danger' in this play is that of incest, which Arbaces comes near to committing with his sister, Panthea. This drives him to a suicidal state from which he is saved in the last act when Gobrias tells him Panthea is not in fact his sister, nor is he the rightful king. Arane, the supposed mother of both – who has been mysteriously pursuing Arbaces's life for many years – knowing the throne needed an heir, had faked a pregnancy; Arbaces, Gobrias's newly-born son was substituted, the queen living to regret this six years later when she found herself really pregnant, with Panthea. An audience which could accept this plot, the outcome of which is darkly hinted at throughout the play, would be making few demands on the playwright apart from ingenuity; furthermore this slender story is padded out with the comedy of Bessus and the swordsmen – an issue which is not only irrelevant to the central plot but detracts from what seriousness and credibility it has. *The Two Noble Kinsmen* (1613–14), by Shakespeare and Fletcher, is an altogether different piece. The audience – whether or not they were familiar with the story from Chaucer's *Knight's Tale* – eagerly waits to see how another triangle of lovers' confusions will be resolved at the end of the play. Beaumont and Fletcher hit on the original idea of keeping Bellario's real identity as a woman a secret until the final scene of *Philaster*, a trick only permissible on the Elizabethan/Jacobean stage and not one capable of repetition (though Jonson employs it – to very different satiric ends – in *Epicoene*). If the dénouement of *A King and No King* is extravagant, it follows Guarinian precedent; that of *The Two Noble Kinsmen* does not. The death of Arcite means that this is in effect a drama with a double outcome, one tragic and one comic, nor is it a less worthy character who dies. The triangle is further complicated by the presence of the Jailer's Daughter, a character drawn from a wholly different sphere, whose love for Palamon is explored and extended in a series of powerful soliloquies tracing her madness and eventual cure. This strikes a more recognizably English note and reveals the native form of tragicomedy finally liberated from its Italian influence and able to make its own original and vital contribution to the development of the genre.

It is possible that Shakespeare collaborated with Fletcher on this play. Certainly the treatment of the Jailer's Daughter shows a sympathy and depth of understanding rare in Fletcher, serving to throw the idealism and heroics of the principal figures into more ironic relief. Since Shakespeare came under the influence of Fletcher, and through him Guarini, it is important to examine his contribution to the tragicomic genre in the light of this. The dramas which are particularly relevant to our study are the romances from *Pericles* to *The Tempest*, written at the end of his career. These plays have many features in common which set them apart from the rest of his work and particularly from the tragedies which immediately preceded them. All are set in a remote time or place and they all include certain fairy-tale elements both in the frequent intervention of supernatural figures and in a less naturalistic attitude to character portrayal and plot development. The plot of all four – *Pericles, Cymbeline, The Winter's Tale* and *The Tempest* – is in embryo substantially the same: a break-up of the family unit leads to separation, banishment (and sometimes death); a period of wandering in exile has the force of a pilgrimage and is rewarded with forgiveness, reconciliation and rebirth. This formula for a drama which moves from tragedy through suffering to a happy outcome is very different from the Italian prototype; indeed it is essentially the material of *King Lear* given a different ending. Shakespeare's source, *The True Chronicle History of King Lear*, reveals the truth of Beaumarchais's argument cited in the previous chapter, for it uses the same story to present a particularly English variety of tragicomedy, differing from Shakespeare's version, as Kenneth Muir amusingly points out, in that 'there is no underplot, no storm, no Fool, no madness and no deaths' (*Shakespeare's Sources*, London, 1957, I, p. 145). The subject-matter is, however, the same and that this historical story was genuinely capable of providing the raw material for a tragicomedy is further revealed in Nahum Tate's 1681 rewrite of the play with a happy ending which held the stage in preference to the original for almost two hundred years.

Before we examine these four plays in detail, however, it is useful to observe that in his earlier comedies Shakespeare gradually evolved a type of drama so mixed in tone as to be a version of tragicomedy. None of his seventeen comedies is unambiguously lighthearted, even *The Comedy of Errors*, framing its Plautine original in the sombre threats on the life of Aegeon. As his career developed Shakespeare tended more and more to bring contrasted genres of tragedy, comedy and history closer together. The second tetralogy of English history plays, in its inclusion of Falstaff and other lowlife companions of Prince Hal, extends the moral potential of the history play into areas undreamt of by the writers of chronicle plays a decade earlier. As the next chapter will examine, the expectations and requirements appropriate to tragedy are challenged and extended by the incorporation of comic material. Even before Shakespeare wrote that group of dramas usually classed as 'dark' or 'problem' comedies (one of which – *Troilus and Cressida* – defied classification by the editors of the First Folio), those comedies written in 1595–1600 go out of their way to combine very contrasted material. The most cursory glance at Shakespeare's sources reveals his determination to extend the conventional bounds of specific dramatic genres, notably in *Much Ado about Nothing*, *Twelfth Night* and *The Merchant of Venice*. In *Much Ado* two different and independent pairs of lovers are contrasted: one pair is almost destroyed by a plot against them, the other is brought together by a plot; the two themes come together and take a tragic turn in the church scene. In *Twelfth Night* the joke against Malvolio, a character outside the central love quartet, is pushed uncomfortably far. That he changes from prose to passionate blank verse in Malvolio's final speech is a mark of the seriousness Shakespeare attaches to the cruelty of the deception. In *The Merchant* the shadow of Shylock darkens the celebrations at Belmont in the last act, serving to expose the cruelty and hypocrisy of the Christians. None of these plays is a tragicomedy according to Guarini's definition. What makes them in essence quite unlike his model is the care Shakespeare takes *not* to graft the plots on one another, *not* to provide a dénouement which brings happiness to all. Shakespeare in these plays prefers juxtaposition to the fusion of opposites, delighting in sharp contrasts of tone rather than over-all unity of mood.

It is particularly rewarding to examine *Measure for Measure* (1603–4) in this context. In fact the five acts fall very closely into the format outlined by Guarini as ideal for tragicomedy, a feature not so much attributable either to imitation or coincidence as to its sources, Cinthio's *Hecatommithi* and his play *Epitia* (themselves powerful influences on Guarini) as well as an English version of the story, Whetstone's *Promos and Cassandra*. The Duke's deter-mination to cleanse Vienna, his appointment of Angelo and the latter's conduct provide the pressing matter which initiates the plot; Act II is principally concerned with the new matters which arise from this, notably Isabella's attempt to save her brother and Angelo's demands; in Act III the Duke is prominent, involved in detailed intrigues to rescue both Isabella and Claudio; in Act IV the issue comes to its tragic climax, the death of Claudio being averted by the fortuitous substitution of Ragozine's head; in the final act all is made clear and the play concludes with the promise of four marriages. Such a neat description of the plotting, how-ever, entirely overlooks precisely what makes this play so original and sets it worlds apart from Guarini's pastoral drama. It also fails to draw attention to precisely those aspects of the play which some literary critics underplay in an attempt to represent the ending as both more just and happier than it inevitably appears on stage. Shakespeare invents the 'bed trick' (whereby one woman substi-tutes herself for another in the dark) – or, rather, borrows it from *All's Well that Ends Well* – in order to save Isabella's honour. Her calm acceptance of this expedient may be seen as offensive, while the Ragozine substitution, another Shakespearian invention, serves to emphasize the weakness of the Duke's scheme. The execution of Barnardine would have saved Claudio but Shake-speare goes beyond all three sources in making the victim un-repentant, with the result that the Duke's plan is saved only by 'an accident that Heaven provides'. The irony of this is made the more pointed through the character and intervention of Lucio, that extension of the medieval Vice, particularly appropriate in this play, who not only pleads with Isabella in the first place and eggs her on in the initial meeting with Angelo, but is a fearless critic of the Duke throughout and in the final scene performs the role of joker, upstaging the Duke and refusing to allow him so neatly to stage-manage and act out his private drama of retribution. Hence the dénouement degenerates from Morality play into farce with the result that we question the appropriateness and value of the neat pairing off. Shakespeare's aim is quite the reverse of Guarini's, his mixture of tragedy and comedy serving to disturb his audience by highlighting the sordid pragmatic realities consequent on the operation of justice.

The great period of Shakespeare's tragic writing grew out of the period in which he produced the problem plays. The last two tragedies, *Antony and Cleopatra* and *Coriolanus*, though pointedly contrasted in terms of dramatic structure, both anticipate the final phase of Shakespeare's writing in that the tragic effects in both plays are minimized. Outside the protagonists, only Enobarbus dies, and of a broken heart: the tragic emotions, raised to such a high pitch in *King Lear*, *Hamlet* and *Macbeth* are already, to employ Guarini's term, tempered. The final plays do not merely have features of narrative and dramatic presentation in common, they reveal a persistent reworking of themes in the attempt to distil something more closely resembling a philosophy of life. Shakespeare's development from *Pericles* to *The Tempest* reveals a struggle to find a theatrical form, a dramatic structure which could not only contain the diversity of genres he was treating, but give them unity, coherence and meaning. In this he was assisted by the neo-classical ideas filtering into English drama via Fletcher, his fellow playwright with the King's Men. The impetus to explore new techniques appeared fortuitously at exactly the same time as Burbage acquired the Blackfriars private theatre. From 1608, for the first time in theatrical history, a professional company played within the city and in a smaller, indoor theatre to a better-educated audience. The élitism of this new drama – a disadvantage where

Fletcher's plays are concerned and in important respects a bad influence on the future development of the English stage – provided Shakespeare towards the end of his career with a challenge to attempt a fresh style and resolve in a new dramatic form those issues which looked beyond tragedy.

Parallels have been drawn between *Philaster* and *Cymbeline*, which were produced at the Globe within the same period. Critics are still undecided as to who influenced whom, a relatively unimportant question when we consider Fletcher's status in the company and the fame he was subsequently to achieve. Certainly the two plays have several features in common. Both have a plot centring on false suspicions of infidelity; both present a faithful mistress disguised as a boy; both are concerned with exile, suffering and a final reconciliation in which all doubts are laid to rest; both contrast the court, where intrigue destroys relationships, with the country which brings the characters closer to nature and a true understanding of each other. In form, theatrical impact and overall objective the two dramas are, however, wholly different. While *Philaster* is a derivative stereotype, *Cymbeline* is one of the most original and unusual plays Shakespeare ever wrote. The awakening of Imogen in the central scene of Act IV illustrates this most clearly. Here is a deliberate attempt to raise emotional horror to its height: the heroine awakens from a drugged sleep to find – as she thinks – the headless body of her husband next to her. She does not know whether this is real or a nightmare. The surreal aspect of the scene is part of the technique of the play as a whole: Shakespeare, taking three quite alien sources, a popular contemporary drama, Holinshed's chronicle and Boccaccio, juxtaposes throughout romance, history and Renaissance intrigue – the Rome of Caius Lucius is separated from that of Iachimo by 1400 years. It is true to say of Shakespeare, as it is not true of Beaumont and Fletcher in *Philaster*, that in this play he sacrifices careful plotting and dramatic technique to the creation of a sensational scene. Imogen's reawakening is bought at a heavy price in terms of theatrical contrivance: it needs a wealth of complicated intrigue to prepare for the scene and in order to extricate himself from this Shakespeare fatally compromises the last act. Bernard Shaw was quite right when he said: 'Unfortunately instead of taking Nature's hint and discarding plots, he borrowed them from all over the place and got into trouble through having to unravel them in the last act, especially in *The Two Gentlemen of Verona* and *Cymbeline*' (Preface, *Cymbeline Refinished*, p. 136).

The final act of *Cymbeline* makes the crucial mistake of presenting a lengthy explanation of facts known not to the characters but to the audience: exactly the opposite of what Guarini advocated. One sympathizes with Shaw who complained that Irving in a production at the Lyceum:

> a statue of romantic melancholy, stood dumb on stage for hours (as it seemed) whilst the others toiled through a series of dénouements of crushing tedium in which the characters lost all their vitality and individuality, and had nothing to do but identify themselves by moles on their necks, or explain why they were not dead.
>
> (p. 134)

Yet Shaw was later to revise his view of the play, realizing that it represented a highly original experiment on Shakespeare's part. It is a far from satisfactory play as a whole: Shakespeare was taking too many risks and he had not yet found the right dramatic form to express his ideas. The intensity of this new vision does flash out, if only intermittently, though most effectively in the awakening scene. Here is a theatrical image of great potency, the full significance of which needed to be worked out through the structure of a whole play. *Cymbeline* represents an advance on *Pericles* in that the haphazard, episodic nature of the narrative in the latter play never attains anything so intense as the images, both verbal and physical, which represent *Cymbeline* at its best. In *The Winter's Tale* (1611) Shakespeare tackled the theme again, this time via his source, Greene's romance *Pandosto*, and produced a more carefully organized drama. Again the dénouement hinges on a miraculous scene of rebirth. Before this the play has alternately plumbed the depths of tragedy and celebrated the heights of comedy. The second half of the play is separated from the first by much more than a sixteen-year gap. In this drama we see most clearly that Shakespeare's art is not one of grafting, but of juxtaposition: source materials, plots, genres, locations are deliberately contrasted. The last act brings these oppositions together – father and child, old friend and enemy, Bohemia and Sicily, country and court, death and rebirth, suffering and reconciliation. They are finally fused, but only at the end of the drama where the many tensions within the vast structure of the play are resolved in one powerful image, the statue of Hermione coming to life: a daring *coup de théâtre* and something quite beyond the art of Guarini.

The Tempest (1611) is structured in a wholly different way, one which has the closest of affinities with the techniques of Guarini. Shakespeare here observes the unities in a way unprecedented in his previous drama: not only do the events take place on the island within the time taken to perform the play, but they *must* do so. Prospero's plot, like Iago's, needs to work quickly or not at all – his 'zenith doth depend upon a most auspicious star'. The first scene throws us into the midst of the action; the rest of the act explains Prospero's 'project', which governs the development of the whole play and prepares us for its shifting moods by presenting alternately scenes which are moving, grotesque, comic, romantic and serious. In Act II Ariel puts into motion Prospero's plan which is complicated when Antonio and Sebastian, unaffected by the music, stay awake and plot to kill Alonso; a further threat to Prospero's scheme is the alliance of Trinculo and Stephano with Caliban. Act III brings the project nearer to a head by imposing labour on Ferdinand, causing Ariel to distract the clowns and confronting the 'three men of sin' with the consequences of their actions. In Act IV it is Prospero's forgetfulness of 'the foul conspiracy' which threatens him with death and almost destroys his plan as surely as it causes the masque, conjured up to celebrate the wedding of Miranda and Ferdinand, to disappear at the end of the act. Prospero's enemies, who all 'lie at his mercy' experience the height of suffering. Shakespeare is so far from making the mistake he did in *Cymbeline* that he surprises his audience with an entirely new twist in the last act: Prospero's decision to renounce his magic, prompted by the sympathy of Ariel for the sufferers. His 'potent art' is relinquished too because of its limited power: Prospero has seen enough setbacks to his scheme and he knows he cannot compel men to be virtuous. He has to resort to blackmail to control Antonio and Sebastian, and force to restrain Caliban: when he returns to Milan 'every third thought shall be my grave' (V. i. 311).

Unimpeded by reliance on any specific narrative source, through observing the three unities and by both extending and refining his own acquired theatrical skills, Shakespeare here produces his most carefully constructed and successful romance. Shakespeare no more needed Guarini to teach him how to write a tragicomedy than Sophocles needed Aristotle to instruct him in the composition of tragedy; but it is not inconceivable that, partly through Shakespeare's association with Fletcher, the ideas of the Italian playwright influenced the writing of this final drama. Whatever the circumstances, the result is a consummate achievement in terms of English tragicomedy. At the climax of the play, through the words of Gonzalo, we are made aware of the unity of the action as it is crystallized in the dénouement:

> O rejoice
> Beyond a common joy! and set it down
> With gold on lasting pillars: in one voyage
> Did Claribel her husband find at Tunis,
> And Ferdinand, her brother, found a wife
> Where he himself was lost, Prospero his dukedom
> In a poor isle, and all of us ourselves
> When no man was his own.

(*The Tempest*, V. i. 206–13)

But Shakespeare combines the neo-classical techniques that enable him to effect a complete fusion of contrasted dramatic genres with his own profound understanding of human nature. He therefore tempers the idyllic ending with a realistic awareness of the weakness of humanity. If we need to define more precisely Shakespeare's objective in this play we can see that it goes well beyond the purging of melancholy. Shakespeare had something very particular to say and he says it in *The Tempest* with absolute precision. His theme, as in all the romances, is pastoral: the conflict of nature and nurture. It is also the overriding issue in *King Lear* in which Shakespeare's analysis led him to reduce mankind to a 'poor bare forked animal'. In the romances, and most triumphantly in *The Tempest*, he invests that nakedness with nobility and hope.

3
Comedy in tragedy: Elizabethan and Jacobean theatre

> *Horatio.*   So shall you hear
>   Of carnal, bloody and unnatural acts;
>   Of accidental judgments, casual slaughters;
>   Of deaths put on by cunning and forc'd cause;
>   And, in this upshot, purposes mistook
>   Fall'n on the inventors' heads.
>
> (*Hamlet*)

If Heminge and Condell found difficulty in assigning some of Shakespeare's plays to exact categories – placing *Troilus and Cressida* between the histories and tragedies while including *Cymbeline* in the tragedies – they would have had the same difficulty with Marlowe. Barabas, the Jew of Malta, represents a particularly vivid reincarnation of the medieval Vice: a bogey figure, alternately dangerous, ludicrous, sympathetic, monstrous. Unlike Shakespeare in his creation of Shylock, Marlowe chooses to sacrifice consistency of character to a deliberate exploitation of contrasted – even contradictory – aspects of the Jew, and in so doing produces a type of play which is very difficult to categorize. The dramatic features of this work make it, therefore, a useful starting-point for a survey of that particularly English blend of comedy and tragedy which contrasts markedly with the Guarini formula. T. S. Eliot drew attention to this originality of tone:

> If one takes *The Jew of Malta* not as a tragedy, or as a 'tragedy of blood' but as a farce, the concluding act becomes intelligible; and if we attend with a careful ear to the versification, we find

that Marlowe develops a tone to suit this farce, and even perhaps that this tone is his most powerful and mature tone. I say farce, but with the enfeebled humour of our times the word is a misnomer; it is the farce of the English humour, the terribly serious, even savage comic humour which spent its last breath in the decadent genius of Dickens.

(*Elizabethan Dramatists*, pp. 63–4)

The 'tragedy of blood', or revenge tragedy, of which *The Jew of Malta* is a powerful and influential example, is a dramatic genre more productive of satire than tragedy and in this sense is an important variation of tragicomedy. We should examine Marlowe's contribution in more detail, as well as comparing it with Shakespeare's theatrical method, before analysing the function of comedy in the more significant revenge plays.

The Jew of Malta (1589/90) becomes comprehensible only if we discard considerations of tragedy; but this is not easy since Barabas at first appears a figure of tragic stature. He is cruelly wronged by the Christians and forced to lose all his money. In standing up to Ferneze and challenging the ethic of the Knights of St John he cuts a far nobler figure than his fellow Jews. His plans for revenge seem just, but in the powerful line, 'A reaching thought will search his deepest wits' (I. ii. 225), Marlowe combines the concepts of Renaissance humanist aspiration and Machiavellian cunning. The Machiavellian, a bogey figure whom Marlowe puts on stage in person as the Prologue to this play, is a further extension of the Vice: he will appear in the form of the many cunning murderers and among the ranks of the malcontents who give this theatrical genre its distinguishing characteristics. At first we are encouraged to approve of Barabas's plan for revenge, but his plot soon leads him into trouble. By involving Ferneze's son Lodovick in a fight with Matthias, during which both are killed, he antagonizes his faithful daughter Abigail, who leaves him. With her our sympathies also depart, a feature clinched by the comic exchange which follows: Abigail, now a Christian convert in earnest – as

distinct from her previously feigned penitence which enabled her
father to regain his secret hoard of money and jewels – forces from
Barabas the enraged response: 'What, Abigail become a nun –
again?' The joke is squarely on him now, as has been shown by
recent productions of the work, which have followed up the pion-
eering criticism of Eliot and, in so doing, revealed the underestimated comic potential both of this play and others in the revenge
genre. Now, as the action develops, the cunning and intrigue into
which Barabas is forced reveal all the features of Guarini's comic
plotting and escalate the play into farce. From being a serious
figure controlling events, Barabas degenerates into a mere pawn,
the victim of the increasingly fraught circumstances which are the
consequence of his earlier act. Thus he becomes more and more of
a figure of fun: he attempts to murder the entire nunnery (to
silence Abigail) and then is forced into the expedient of killing the
two friars through a subterfuge deliberately recalling – and par-
odying – the feigned challenge to Lodovick and Matthias. Abigail
has significantly been replaced in his affections by Ithamore, a
very different figure, grotesque and untrustworthy. When Ithamore becomes involved with the courtesan Bellamira, Barabas has
to resort to the farcical expedient of the poisoned nosegay and the
no less ludicrous disguise of a French musician to poison them.
Finally, outmanoeuvred even after feigning death, he falls victim
to his own cunning scheme and ends up in the cauldron he had
prepared for Ferneze.

The elimination of Barabas represents not so much a dénouement of the action as a savagely comic *coup de théâtre* which is the
ultimate expression of the ambivalence to the character throughout, a reflection of the Elizabethan attitude to Jews: part terror and
part derision. Such a volatile mix of dramatic elements seeks to
exploit the emotional composition of the audience: in no sense is
Marlowe seeking an Aristotelian purgation through pity and fear.
The comedy is dangerous and unpredictable. An echo of this anti-
Semitism is heard in *Doctor Faustus* (1592/3) when – in the shorter
version of the 1604 Quarto – the Horse-Corser, punning in his

reference to 'Doctor Lupus', alludes to the execution of Doctor Lopez, the Queen's Jewish physician, who was falsely accused of attempting to poison her. Since this event took place in 1594, the year after Marlowe was murdered, such an interpolated topical joke illustrates that licence given to clowns to improvise which prompts Hamlet's advice to the players. A further feature of significance – apart from the discrediting of the authority of the 1604 Quarto – is that such comic ad libbing should occur in a tragedy. In the plays of this period serious issues go alongside scenes of knockabout clowning and it is important to understand to what extent such a mixture represented a potentially irresponsible undermining of the audience's involvement and to what extent, in the hands of a skilful dramatist, it can be utilized to extend the whole range and scope of the play. No play provides a finer example than *Doctor Faustus* of the careful integration and employment of comic techniques in tragedy; and since Marlowe has been given little credit for his originality, his dramatic method here is worthy of more detailed examination.

It is unfortunate that the establishing of the superiority of the longer 'B' text of 1616 over the shorter 'A' text of 1604 by W. W. Greg in his 1950 edition has still not had its full effect, notably in theatrical performance, the argument being further complicated by an unwillingness to accept Marlowe's hand in the comic scenes. Whether he was fully responsible for the dialogue throughout is, in any case, relatively unimportant since the comic scenes were in several respects improvisatory. What is important is that he devised a very careful scenario which causes the comic scenes to function in a very precise way within the wider scope of this serious drama. Critics have drawn attention to the element of parody in the first two acts which throughout juxtapose serious scenes involving 'great' public figures with comic interludes concerning the antics of low-life clowns. Marlowe's technique in Acts III and IV extends this straightforward contrast into a far more elaborate and subtle structure, which can be represented as follows:

(A) CHORUS I:
    Rome   (1): Bruno, the anti-Pope, is spirited away.
               (2): Knockabout farce: Pope baiting.
    comic scene: Vintner and Mephostophilis.

(B) CHORUS II:
    Germany (1): Entertainment for Charles V.
               (2): Cheap revenge: the taunting of Benvolio.
    comic scene: Horse-Corser.
    comic scene: meeting of all the clowns in the inn.

(C) Vanholt: conjuring for the Duchess is interrupted by the clowns.

Marlowe's aim in the first two acts is to reveal the irony of Faustus's committing himself to the Devil; this he achieves essentially through parody: in Wagner's treatment of the scholars, his binding of Robin to serve him, and in Robin's determination to exploit magic for pleasure. In Acts III and IV he wishes to emphasize the way in which Faustus's stature is gradually reduced as he fritters away his twenty-four years, and the patterning of these scenes points clearly to this. A chorus establishes a lofty tone which is present in the succeeding scene but gradually gives way to a pathetic contrast with trivial action. This is reinforced by the low-life comic scene which follows. Marlowe repeats this sequence in Germany and then telescopes it in the one scene in Vanholt. Gradually throughout the three parts of this central section of the play not only is Faustus's achievement belittled (he falls from involvement in a serious religious and political conflict to fetching grapes for a pregnant duchess) but he becomes at the same time more directly involved with the clowns. They distract Mephostophilis from his service, cause him to play a childish prank on the Horse-Corser, discuss his conduct – in the powerful alienation effect provided by the inn scene – and finally burst in to the court at Vanholt to confront him with the waste of his talents, a reality he methodically (and symbolically) silences. Thus figures from an alien world of comedy – whose own stature is more acutely diminished throughout in a declension which moves from Wagner through Robin and Dick to the Horse-Corser – are employed to undermine the gravity of the main plot and its protagonist. Marlowe, having here countered Sidney's accusation that playwrights carelessly mingle clowns and kings and having no further use for those figures who have now fulfilled their dramatic function, returns in Act V to the serious Morality structure of the play.

Marlowe's integration of serious and comic material influenced Shakespeare most noticeably in his writing of the second historical tetralogy; in the field of tragedy he works differently. His technique is less formalized and it differs from play to play as he explored the rich possibilities of this interrelation of contrasted genres. The more straightforward Aristotelian structure of *Othello* and *Coriolanus* precludes any extensive comic effects; so does the tight structure of his shortest tragedy, *Macbeth*, with the vital exception of the Porter's scene, in which Shakespeare allows the audience a breathing-space immediately after the murder of Duncan and before its consequences are revealed. This comic scene represents a particularly sharp and sudden change of mood, but, through its harping on the theme of equivocation, a central issue in the play as a whole, it does not break the continuity of the drama. It is carefully employed as a brake on the emotional pressures which at this point have built to such a high pitch that they must be relaxed before the next stage of the drama can develop. Comedy is employed far more extensively in the wider canvas of *King Lear* (1603–6). The play contains three contrasted madmen: one a professional fool, part court entertainer, part 'natural', part bitter conscience; one a man assuming the character of a 'Bedlam beggar' to avoid arrest; the other – the protagonist himself – a man who through the consequences of his own arrogant folly is driven insane. Far from acting as a sort of lightning conductor to deflect any potentially risible effects away from the dignity of Lear, the fool undermines his master's tragic stature on the heath, making us aware that his conduct is merely wilful, his language little more than rant. Later the situation will become far more complex as

Shakespeare in one scene only (III. vi) brings all three together. The result is an onslaught on the audience's feelings unparalleled in the rest of his work. We are not allowed the comfortable purgation of tears; rather, Shakespeare gets under our skin by forcing us simultaneously to sympathize with the characters and yet think through the complex emotional and philosophical issues brought here to a head. The scene marks a decisive turning-point in the main plot: the fool henceforth disappears and Edgar drops his disguise as Mad Tom. Shakespeare has taken us as far as he dares in appealing at one and the same time to our emotive and rational faculties. Brecht said, 'Sorrow is hostile to thought; it stifles it; and thought is hostile to sorrow' (*Messingkauf Dialogues*, p. 47); Shakespeare anticipated (and influenced) Brecht's concept of Epic Theatre in his refusal here to draw the audience into a straightforward cathartic experience.

Comedy features very differently in *Antony and Cleopatra* (1606/7). In contrast to the carefully worked-out plot of *Coriolanus* which leads inevitably to the peripeteia and its recognition in the hero's cry: 'O mother, mother, what have you done?' after which he 'holds her by the hand, silent' (V. iii. 182), Shakespeare's other late Roman play observes none of Aristotle's precepts. The ignobility of the hero is insisted on from the first line, the action shifts backwards and forwards between Rome and Alexandria, Antony dies in Act IV. Antony's death scene is so presented as to constitute a mixture of effects which may be described as tragicomic. It is not only the ironies of Eros's suicide and Antony's bungled attempt – both brought about by Cleopatra's misguided trick of feigning death in order to win him back – which introduce a comic note; this is extended in the next scene as the guards, expressing the noblest of choric sentiments, fail to assist him. In the scene which follows Cleopatra dares not leave the monument and consequently Antony has to be drawn up to her. The clumsiness of this is exploited by Shakespeare in the staging which deliberately deflates many of the tragic expressions of both protagonists. Critics who fail to observe a humour in this scene are insufficiently aware of the impossibility of carrying it off on a stage like the Globe without loss of dignity, and choose to overlook its fundamental purpose: a preparation for the equivocal conduct of the heroine in the last act as she singularly fails to live up to her protestations of loyalty consequent on Antony's death. Shakespeare is not here presenting a satiric portrait in the vein of *Troilus and Cressida*; rather, he is extending the potential of tragedy by making us aware that his protagonists are human. By showing the gap between heroism and more down-to-earth concerns he expands the range of our emotional sympathies for the characters.

Finally a consideration of *Hamlet* (1601/2) leads to an examination of the genre of revenge tragedy, which is tragicomic in essence. The revenger's position is in existential terms an absurd one: he is forced to listen to two contradictory codes, the demand for revenge and the Christian ethic. Hamlet is no exception, though his vacillation is brought about by something more complex even than this: his basic inability to accept the validity of any action. Moreover, were Hamlet to kill the king, he could not then see the realization of that deeper motive: the desire to have his mother repent by rejecting Claudius. He is forced to stall, his conduct being a reflection of the depth of the irony in his promise to the Ghost that 'I with wings as swift / As meditation or the thoughts of love / May sweep to my revenge' (I. v. 29–31). The antic disposition he adopts gives rise to a considerable amount of comedy, the tone of which varies according to the extent to which Hamlet is genuinely in control of this impersonation. Shakespeare extends the central ironies of the situation by contrasting Hamlet's revenge plot with that of Laertes, and his madness with that of Ophelia. The scheming, expressed in the complex intrigues of the various spies which characterizes Act III, gives way to a presentation of the consequences of Hamlet's actions in the fourth act: the madness and death of Ophelia and Laertes's plan for revenge. The last act, opening with the grim comedy of the graveyard scene, almost literally and to powerful theatrical effect, matches hornpipes and funerals, and culminates in the final blood-bath. It is this feature of the play and of the revenge convention which most strongly emphasizes its tragicomic potential. Instead of developing towards Aristotle's *anagnorisis* whereby the hero at his death experiences enlightenment in one powerful climactic moment, the revenge play ends with the confounding of carefully laid schemes – in theory and very often in effect the stuff of comedy. As the genre developed in the first two decades of the seventeenth century, its more ambiguous features – the revenger's motives, methods and achievement, inherent in the format of Thomas Kyd's *The Spanish Tragedy* and opened up in *Hamlet* – were to be taken to increasingly greater extremes.

Tourneur's *The Revenger's Tragedy* (*c.* 1606) extracts the maximum of comedy from the genre without introducing characters outside the world of the court. The names of the Duke's sons, Lussurioso, Ambitioso, Supervacuo and Spurio, go beyond any simple association with Morality figures and prepare us for Tourneur's emphasis on the unfolding of the action. The murder of the Duke in Act III is fully representative of the grotesque tone of the play, Vendice going out of his way to find both a cunningly appropriate death and location for the murder. The consequences of this further complicate the ingenious plotting which takes on a pronounced comic note as Vendice, having dropped his disguise as Piato, is reintroduced to Lussurioso who engages him to murder the missing man: a dilemma he neatly solves by fixing the blame for the Duke's murder on Piato himself. Super-subtle scheming throughout the play edges the drama towards farce, as when Vendice manages to get Lussurioso imprisoned for mistakenly assaulting his father and mother or when the plot of the two step-brothers misfires, bringing about the death of their own brother instead. The way Tourneur handles this leads to a high point of comedy in the play:

> *Ambitioso.* O death and vengeance!
> *Supervacuo.* Hell and torments!
> *Ambitioso.* Slave, camest thou to delude us?

Officer. Delude you, my lords?
Supervacuo. Ay, villain, where's his head now?
Officer. Why here, my lord;
    Just after his delivery, you both came
    With warrant from the duke to behead your brother.
Ambitioso. Ay, our brother, the duke's son.
Officer. The duke's son, my lord, had his release before you
    came.
Ambitioso. Whose head's that then?

(III. v. 69–79)

Moreover, the final destruction of the corrupt court does not go as planned. Vendice's masque of revengers is doubled – and effectively parodied – by the other masque of intended murderers, the sheer excess of which, resulting in the hectic sequence of stabbings, renders the dénouement ludicrous. Tourneur's intentions in this play are essentially frivolous; the audience take nothing to heart. Critics who insist that the play is a moral indictment of vice, have paid too little attention to Tourneur's skilful deflecting of the more disturbing aspects of the genre in his handling of the plot throughout.

Tourneur's technique and theatrical aim are very different from Webster's whose two tragedies, *The Duchess of Malfi* and *The White Devil*, are shot through with flashes of comedy which serve both to illuminate the situation and to penetrate more deeply and disturbingly into our consciousness. There is nothing facile about Webster's theatrical effects. Though the plotting may at times strain the credulity of a modern audience which requires a greater consistency of psychology, Bernard Shaw's dismissive expression, 'a mere Tussaud laureate' (*Our Theatre in the Nineties*, III, p. 317), does no justice to Webster's philosophical and ethical purpose. *The Duchess of Malfi* (1612–14) extends that mixture of comedy and tragedy basic to the genre in its juxtaposition of scheming and emotional danger by contrasting the scheming of the malcontent Bosola, which in Act III results in the Duchess's fatal confession to him of her secret marriage, with the protracted torments of Act IV which culminate in her death. The masque which Ferdinand presents is a grimly ironic entertainment, an extended parody of an epithalamium, employing all its traditional features: the introduction of the masquers, their entry, a dance, the 'taking out' of the noble figure by the revellers, the presentation of gifts and the final song. All of this is performed by madmen, directed by the presenter, Bosola: an original theatrical twist which serves simultaneously to intensify and distance the horror. In *The White Devil* (*c.* 1611) too the protagonist is finally killed by her enemies who announce: 'We have brought you a masque!' (V. vi. 189). In this play Webster extracts every ounce of savage humour from the tragic events. The first two murders – of Isabella and Camillo – are performed in dumb show, the ingeniousness of their execution being underlined by the respective comments of Brachiano: 'Excellent, then she's dead' (II. ii. 24) and 'T'was quaintly done' (II. ii. 38). The play acting, which has constantly been a major feature of the genre from Hieronymo's presentation of his drama *Soliman and Perseda*, in which he carefully allots the leading roles to his enemies and friends, through to Hamlet's assumption of an 'antic disposition', is carried to its ultimate in *The White Devil*. Flamineo's trick to test his sister results in his mock death and startling resurrection but this joke immediately gives way to a more ghastly reality as they are surprised by Lodovico and Gasparo. Even as he and Vittoria are stabbed, Flamineo can ask: 'O what blade is't / A Toledo or an English fox?' (V. vi. 234–5) and, as he dies, jest about death: 'I have caught / An everlasting cold. I have lost my voice / Most irrevocably' (V. vi. 270–2). It is the outrageousness of these verbal conceits, matched throughout the play by equally striking theatrical effects, which reveal most clearly Webster's moral aim in bringing his audience as well as his characters to a closer awareness of mortality.

Middleton and Rowley's *The Changeling* (1622) brings the development from Marlowe full circle in that this play represents a conscious attempt to integrate a sequence of carefully worked-out comic scenes with the main tragic plot. Middleton's moral story (of the corruption of his heroine Beatrice-Joanna who gradually becomes more dependent on De Flores, the 'wondrous necessary man', who has murdered her intended husband in order that she may marry Alsemero) is matched point by point by the comic invention of Rowley who presents a parody in which Alibius, a jealous old doctor, entrusts the virtue of his young wife to the care of his servant, Lollio. Here the sub-plot deals with an alien world of comic characters whose conduct in large part is governed by the conventions of the *commedia dell'arte*. It has the effect of throwing the action of Middleton's noble characters into ironic relief and making them all appear as mad as the inmates of Alibius's asylum. More recent productions of the play which have given due attention to the Rowley plot – or indeed have inverted the two by setting the main action in the asylum – have drawn attention to the satiric purpose of the play in its exposure of sin and guilt. The potentially tragic stature of the protagonists is further reduced by the careful drawing together of the two plots at the end and the pointed parallels made between them. Rather than finding the tragedy diminished by the sub-plot, however, we discover that the moral potential of the drama is extended by this harsh juxtaposition of serious and comic material.

Comedy is most strongly in evidence in Marston's *The Malcontent* (1602/3) which goes to great pains to convert the conventional formula of revenge drama into a play with an unambiguously happy outcome. Altofronto lacks both the sexual motivation of Ferdinand and Hamlet's duty to avenge the death of a kinsman. He is closer to Prospero in that the restoration of his usurped dukedom is his prime objective. Indeed, in the play revenge seems at times something of an afterthought, as in this exchange:

> *Malevole.* A cuckold! To be a thing that's hoodwinked with kindness whilst every rascal fillips his brows; to have a coxcomb with egregious horns pinn'd to a lord's back, every page sporting himself with delightful laughter, whilst he must be the last must know it.

Pistols and poniards! Pistols and poniards!
Pietro. Death and damnation!
Malevole. Lightning and thunder!
Pietro. Vengeance and torture!
Malevole. Catzo!
Pietro. O, revenge!

(I. iii. 94–104)

The comic extravagance of the language here is entirely characteristic of the play. The verbal ingenuity of Malevole is emphasized, not any dangerous physical consequences of his wit. Malevole achieves his aim with virtually as little bloodshed as Prospero, the one moment of violence which results in the apparent death of Ferneze being turned to Malevole's advantage when the duke surprisingly revives. The scenes of pure comedy – involving Bilioso, Biancha, Passarello and Maquerelle – complement rather than undermine the serious plot. Marston relishes the disguises and reveals the inherently ridiculous element in the dramatic representation of murder by cunning in the scene where Malevole appears to be 'poisoned with an empty box'. In pushing the relentlessness of the intrigue to its logical conclusion, Marston exposes this basically comic aspect of the genre, notably in the sequence of short scenes in which Pietro, having – in the improbable disguise of the Hermit of the Rock – narrated his own death, is persuaded by Mendoza to murder Malevole whilst the latter is at the same time ordered to kill Pietro. Characters like Aurelia and Pietro conveniently repent or are outmanoeuvred, as in the climactic masque which inverts the conventional function of such an entertainment in revenge plays by restoring the two dukes to their wives instead of bringing about their destruction. In exploiting to the full the comic implications of the genre Marston creates a drama which is a perfect burlesque not merely of the revenge play but of the Guarinian model for tragicomedy.

4

French seventeenth-century tragicomedy

> *Chimène.* Malgré les feux si beaux, qui troublent ma colère,
>   Je ferai mon possible à bien venger mon père;
>   Mais malgré la rigueur d'un si cruel devoir,
>   Mon unique souhait est de ne rien pouvoir.
> *Don Rodrigue.* O miracle d'amour!
> *Chimène.*   O comble de misères!
> *Don Rodrigue.* Que de maux et de pleurs nous coûterons nos
>   pères!
> *Chimène.* Rodrigue, qui l'eût cru?
> *Don Rodrigue.*   Chimène, qui l'eût dit?
> *Chimène.* Que notre heure fût si proche et sitôt se perdît?
>   (Pierre Corneille, *Le Cid*)

When Corneille completed his drama *Le Cid* in 1636 he called it a tragicomedy, although there is nothing comic about the play. It gave rise to a celebrated and bitter literary debate when it was attacked by Scudéry in his *Observations sur 'Le Cid'* in April 1637 and the issue was subsequently referred to the French Académie after Corneille had defended his play in a *Lettre apologétique*. The Académie, while considering Scudéry's criticisms excessive – he objected to the construction of the play, its breaking of the dramatic rules, its bad versification and its plagiarism – nevertheless conceded that *Le Cid* did not observe with sufficient care the neoclassical concept of the three unities (of time, place and action) derived from Aristotle via the translation of his *Poetics* by Castelvetro in 1570. Corneille himself was never able to forget this criticism, so much more than academic in its effect on his reputation and career, returning to the fight with his *Discours des Trois Unités* in 1660. The decision of the Académie had wider repercussions, not only on his drama but on that of his contemporaries and successors. Corneille wrote other plays which though they were termed tragedies have none of the features Aristotle regarded as vital to the genre; like *Le Cid* they avoid a fatal outcome but in their tighter construction and increased economy of theatrical effects they both served to answer the criticism levelled at *Le Cid* and influenced the work of later writers.

English theatre has never been subject to the criticisms and repression of a literary organization with the power of the French Académie, nor has it ever been seriously influenced by such a rigid (and inaccurate) interpretation of classical rules as that represented by the concept of the three unities. Dryden's attitude is entirely characteristic: in the essay *Of Dramatick Poesie*, though Crites, speaking for the Ancients, expounds a theory similar to that held by the Académie, a little later Eugenius comments:

> The Unity of Place, however it might be practised by them, was never any of their rules: We find it neither in Aristotle, Horace or any who have written of it, till in our age the French poets first made it a precept of the stage.

(p. 55)

Dryden himself experimented with the unities, but never felt himself constrained by them. In *All for Love* he reduces the characters to ten and sets the action within one day in the palace at Alexandria; but in *The Tempest* he chooses entirely to disregard Shakespeare's careful observation of all three unities. From the seventeenth century to the present day the respect for classical precedent and rules has strongly affected the French threatre. Order, control, restraint were the distinguishing features of the *grand siècle*. The seventeenth century in England, however, was not an age of peace. It saw the execution of one monarch and the dethronement of another: social and political turbulence which was reflected alike in the satire of the Jacobean stage and the mordant wit of the Restoration dramatists. French drama, so long in the shadow of Richelieu, portrayed a very different society from that which emerges in all its sexual and mercenary unscrupulousness in the drama of Wycherley. The period of Charles II was not a heroic age as was that of Louis XIV; not until civil war gave way to victorious conquest abroad in the reign of Queen Anne did England find stability. In France the philosophers of reason, Descartes and Pascal, stand alongside Corneille, Molière and Racine whose attitudes to theatre they shared and influenced.

Drama by its very nature thrives on conflict and in a turbulent era will find ample material for the stage. But the French were unique in discovering and developing a dramatic form which in the seventeenth century corresponded closely to the order they observed and respected. Their theatre did not ignore the destructive reality of passion nor the equally potent horror of a calmly reasoned existence. The plays of Racine are so often concerned with the former, while a work like Molière's *Dom Juan* gives powerful expression to the latter. Between these two extremes is another type of drama, the tragicomedy, which was particularly suited to exploring that 'regulated tug-of-war' which Martin Turnell sees as the essential feature of French life and theatre in this period:

> Neither 'reason' nor 'passion' alone is sufficient to produce 'the good life'. A man who is at the mercy of his passions falls into anarchy, but the man who eliminates or tries to eliminate them altogether is condemned to sterility. A perfect balance between the two is equally unacceptable as a solution because it produces the *plein repos* which opens the door to 'weariness, gloom, sadness, fretfulness, vexation' and finally 'despair' (a quotation from the *Pensées* of Pascal) which bring him by a different but not less certain route to the abyss.

> The only healthy condition is a regulated tug-of-war. The peculiar vitality of French literature in the seventeenth century lies in a very delicate poise between 'reason' and 'passion', in a sense of tension and repose which is quite different from the

tension of the English writers and which is the result of an ambivalent attitude towards authority. Authority is not accepted passively. It is accepted and resisted, and it is this that gives the literature its life, its high degree of emotional vitality combined with a high degree of order.

(*The Classical Moment*, pp. 14–15)

Dryden's Neander might well find Corneille's *Cinna* and *Pompey* 'not so properly to be called Plays, as long discourses of State' and his *Polyeucte* 'in matters of Religion . . . as solemn as the long stops upon our Organs' (*Of Dramatick Poesie*, p. 79). The concept of what constituted powerful drama in seventeenth-century France was as far removed from what pleased the English as Dryden's wit was from the studied verses of Corneille. Elsewhere Corneille's tragicomedies are given more credit by Lisideius, but they were to prove supremely uncopiable, a far greater achievement than the heroic tragedies, shot through with ironic observation, which represent the most serious endeavours of the contemporary English stage.

Le Cid, despite the hostility with which it was received, has remained Corneille's best-known and most frequently performed work. One of the reasons for this is the vitality consequent on the amount of action in the play. It was adapted by Corneille from a drama by Guillen de Castro published in 1618, a work which, like the plays of the English Renaissance, crams a welter of events into its sprawling canvas. Corneille was obliged to select the key events from the story but was still left with the problem of cramming two duels, two clandestine visits from the hero to his mistress and a battle with the Moors into the formula prescribed by the Académie's insistence on observation of the unities. He bent the rules in a way which proved unsatisfactory to his critics; the ingenuity of his solution is more evident than the resolution of the theatrical problem. There is far more action in this play than in any of his subsequent dramas, a fault he was to amend later by moving towards a more concentrated inevitability of plot, one dependent on character rather than circumstances or incident. In the first scene of *Le Cid*, Chimène gratefully receives the news that her father favours Rodrigue as her suitor. Her happiness is dashed when the fathers of the two young people get involved in an argument: this forces Rodrigue into fighting a duel against Chimène's father. This confronts the hero at the end of the first act with the dilemma central to all Corneille's plays: the struggle between love and duty. At the heart of his drama is that conflict between passion and reason which expresses itself in the opposition of a thesis and an antithesis which during a debate – either in soliloquy or with another character – will find a synthesis indicating a new and more complex attitude to life. This is the authentic heroic note in Corneille and is the essence of his concept of tragicomedy.

Rodrigue's soliloquy which closes the act is a *tour de force* of rhetoric, set not in alexandrines, like the rest of the play, but in carefully modulated stanza form. This sudden change of style – which displeased Scudéry – is a high point of the drama in which conflicting emotions are confronted and resolved. The first stanza conveys numbed horror at the sudden turn of events and the hero's inability to appreciate the full force of his misfortune. In the second stanza the issues begin to clarify themselves; though the repeated phrase 'O dieu, l'étrange peine' harks back to the initial shock, Rodrigue recognizes the grim truth of the situation. The third stanza, concentrating on the image of his sword – a physical reality on the stage – gives more precise expression to his dilemma: that in revenging his honour he must lose his mistress. This leads in the next verse to the contemplation of suicide which seems at first an easy way out, but is soon rejected as an ignoble act. The development of his thoughts is counterpointed with the relentlessly repeated refrain of the last line which, with every new verse, serves to recall the insult to his father and the inevitability of losing Chimène. The final stanza brings the conflicting issues to a conclusion in a precisely formulated expression of his newly found determination to follow a course of action which has emerged from the gradual clarification of the opposed values as blinding passion has slowly been distanced and held in check by a new awareness born of the exercise of reason:

> Oui, mon esprit s'était déçu.
> Je dois tout à mon père avant qu'à ma maîtresse:
> Que je meure au combat, ou meure de tristesse,
> Je rendrai mon sang pûr comme je l'ai reçu.
> Je m'accuse déjà de trop de négligence:
> Courons à la vengeance;
> Et tout honteux d'avoir tout balancé
> Ne soyons plus en peine,
> Puisqu'aujourd-hui mon père est offensé
> Si l'offenseur est père de Chimène.

> Yes, I was wrong.
> My duty's to my father, not to her.
> Whether I die from sword or broken heart,
> I'll shed my blood as pure as at my birth.
> I tax myself with being too remiss.
> Let's hasten to revenge;
> Deeply ashamed at having wavered so,
> Let's hesitate no more,
> Since it's my father who's offended, and
> Ximena's father has offended him.

> (*Le Cid*, I. vi. 341–50)

The last two lines cleverly echo the end of the first stanza almost exactly, but the alteration of the emphasis underlines Rodrigue's conversion from emotional victim to a man in control of himself and events. The resolution of the hero's dilemma here is entirely characteristic of Corneille's technique throughout the drama. This marks only the first stage in that synthesis which is effected in the wider canvas of the play; Rodrigue's determination, though it imposes order on his confused emotions and thoughts, will lead to the duel, the death of the count and a further, more terrible dilemma for himself and Chimène. His development during the five acts of the drama mirrors the progress charted in the soliloquy here. He first goes to her demanding that she kill him and then in the second interview, after he has defeated the Moors, tells her he thinks of the final duel with Don Sanche as his execution: suicide still seems the noblest solution. But as Chimène in their first scene together tells him she cannot hate him, and in their last meeting more openly confesses her love for him, telling him he owes it to her to defeat his rival, so the drama slowly converts tragedy to tragicomedy. Scudéry objected to the fact that Corneille had betrayed the basic principle of tragicomedy by giving away the outcome of the action early in the play. There are strong echoes of Guarini in his insistence that:

> Because it is a mixture of tragedy and comedy and because in its dénouement it tends more to the latter, it is important that in this type of writing the first act should set underway an intrigue which maintains the suspense throughout and which is not unravelled until the end of the work. . . . It does not need an Alexander to undo the Gordian knot of *Le Cid*; the least clairvoyant of the audience can guess or even see the end of this adventure as soon as it has begun.
>
> (*Le Cid*, p. 114)

This seems neither fair nor to the point. It is not at all clear how the plot will be resolved: even in the last act Corneille creates suspense when it is Don Sanche who returns from the duel to the dismay of Chimène; she does not realize that Rodrigue, the victor, magnanimously spared his life. What is more important is that Corneille has structured the play in such a way as to make the denouement inevitable and yet unexpected. The inevitability resides in the gradual surmounting of the obstacles to Chimène's marriage to Rodrigue, the unexpected in the way this is effected. When Rodrigue demands that Chimène plunge his sword in his breast this is not the empty rhetorical flourish of Shakespeare's Richard III before Lady Anne: he is speaking in earnest and though she cannot kill him, neither can she renounce her vendetta.

That is, not until Rodrigue's victory over the Moors makes him indispensable to the state, when the king can read Chimène's true thoughts and can counter her demand for a champion with the insistence that she must marry whoever wins the duel.

Her dilemma may seem unreal and her objections to Rodrigue insincere; but they are not, nor can the resolution be easy. It is more reasonable to object that she passes through too absolute and unbelievable a conversion within the space of twenty-four hours, but the fault here is more with the inflexibility of the Académie than with the playwright. As Dryden pointed out, quoting Corneille:

> I will alledge Corneille's words, as I find them in the end of his Discourse of the Three Unities: 'il est facile aux speculatifs d'estre sevères, etc'. 'Tis easie for speculative persons to judge severely; but if they would produce to publick view ten or twelve pieces of this nature, they would perhaps give more latitude to the rules than I have done, when by experience they had known how much we are limited and constrained by them, and how many beauties of the Stage they banish from it.
>
> (*Of Dramatick Poesie*, p. 83)

It is also significant that in this play Corneille motivates the conversion from tragedy to a happy outcome largely through external circumstances and an imposed design. Both Chimène and Rodrigue are consistent, but they would remain indissolubly locked in permanent conflict were it not for his defeat of the Moors and the inevitable sequence of events which this gives rise to. Moreover, their dilemma is forced on them in the first place by the conduct of their fathers. In the plays he wrote after *Le Cid* Corneille sought to avoid these problems by making the characters more responsible for their own actions and by more carefully organizing the resolution of the dilemma. The chief dramatic weakness of *Le Cid* is its failure to observe the unity of action, the central requirement of Aristotle's thesis. The plot is set underway by two characters – the fathers – who are outside the central conflict, and it is resolved as a result of Rodrigue's victory which is the subject of a lengthy narrative, essentially a digression. This weakness is exacerbated by Corneille's concern with a character who has nothing whatsoever to do with the main plot: the Infanta. Her situation, moreover, makes it far more difficult to accept Chimène's. She is both a more sympathetic and a more heroic figure, in love herself with Rodrigue but determined to control her passion. She it was who introduced him to Chimène: 'J'ai allumé leurs feux pour éteindre les miens (I lit their fires of love to put out mine)' (I. ii. 104) she points out to her confidante, Léonore. It is in her first scene that we see more clearly that balance between emotion and reason which will characterize Corneille's later heroines. Here it is more immediately productive of an extended pathos, an almost masochistic dwelling on the mixture of pain and pleasure which is nevertheless kept in tight control:

> Si l'amour vit d'espoir, il périt avec lui:
> C'est un feu qui s'éteint, faute de nourriture;
> Et malgré la rigueur de ma triste aventure,
> Si Chimène a jamais Rodrigue pour mari,
> Mon espérance est morte et mon esprit guéri.
> Je souffre cependant un tourment incroyable.

> Love lives on hope but perishes with it;
> It is a fire that dies for lack of food;
> Despite the harshness of my destiny
> If my Rodrigue and Ximena wed,
> I shall be dead to hope but live at peace.
> Meanwhile my torments are beyond belief.

(II. ii. 108–13)

The final line is the key: painful conflict between personal feelings and duty is subtly maintained throughout the play, every twist of the central action giving the Infanta renewed hope and with it an added determination to repress her illicit love.

With *Cinna* (1640) Corneille sought to counter those who

objected to the defective dramatic technique of *Le Cid*. It is a far more concentrated play opening with an impassioned soliloquy by Emilie which immediately establishes the central conflict: of love and hatred, of concern for Cinna but duty to her father. In *Le Cid* Corneille made the mistake of initiating a series of actions in the first act which lead to a plethora of incidents awkwardly crammed into a short space of time. He does precisely the opposite in *Cinna*, beginning on the eve of the assassination of Auguste and making us aware that the situation is one which has been maturing for many years. He has learnt to restrict the action to the past and to concentrate instead on the final stage of the conflict, a technique Shakespeare perfected in *The Tempest*. For this reason Emilie's predicament is more acceptable than Chimène's. Hatred of Auguste's tyranny, duty to her murdered father and love for Cinna are all long-standing; now what gives these contrasted feelings added focus and intensity is the fear that her lover may lose his life. Emilie's dilemma has a parallel in that of all the other principal characters, a quartet who are all intimately involved in the same central situation. Cinna is torn between his love of Emilie and his affection for Auguste, Maxime between his loyalty to Cinna and his own passion for Emilie, Auguste himself between personal and state affairs. Throughout the drama the tension never relaxes. Corneille, after establishing the initial circumstances, presents us with a scene in which Auguste asks Cinna and Maxime if he is right to abdicate, thus placing them both in an ironic situation and forcing Cinna to argue against the suggestion since he can only prove his love for Emilie by killing the emperor. Cinna's subsequent reservations, however, give rise to the confrontation with Emilie in which she threatens to kill both Auguste and herself if he is not adamant. Maxime is the catalyst in the action: his betrayal of Cinna precipitates the climax in which Auguste confronts the rebel and then, when he finds Emilie prepared to die with him, is moved to compassion and, on the advice of Livie, pardons them. Hence Maxime's scheme leads not to a tragic outcome but to clemency and reconciliation, he himself expressing contrition in the final act.

Corneille expressed his preference for the type of drama which ended happily and though he called *Cinna* a tragedy, it is in fact much closer to tragicomedy than the tragedy with a happy ending discussed by Aristotle and emulated by sixteenth-century writers in Italy. In the 'Discours du poème dramatique' he says:

> It is a fact that we never see a noble figure (honnête homme) on our stage without wishing him to be prosperous and feeling displeased at his misfortune. This means that when he is brought low we leave the theatre with regret and take away something resembling indignation towards the author and the actors; but when the outcome fulfils our hopes and when virtue is crowned with reward we leave joyful, totally satisfied both with the play and those who have acted it.
>
> (*Théâtre Complet*, I, p. 11)

With *Polyeucte* (1642) he created another drama in which contrasted values are balanced throughout and consequently the tragic catastrophe is avoided. Yet this play ends with the death of the hero, executed for his Christian sympathies. His death, however, is seen as a martyrdom: in no sense tragic, but rather an inspiration for all the characters to renounce their paganism and learn by his example. Again the most fascinating figure is the heroine, Pauline, since she it is who most fully suffers the conflict of opposed feelings and finally triumphs through the exercise of will. The play opens with a reference to her dream; again past events determine the course of the drama, the dream giving vivid focus to her twin fears: that her husband will die and her old lover return. In both this play and *Cinna* Corneille managed to avoid the problems which derive essentially from his source in *Le Cid*. His inspiration here was a sixteenth-century *Vitae Sanctorum* by a German friar, while for Cinna he drew on the *De Clementia* of Seneca; hence he was free to invent his own action and to concentrate on telling confrontations. Again the play maintains its tension to the end, Polyeucte's adamant refusal to compromise being matched by Pauline's nobility, her heroic 'générosité' in fighting to protect her husband rather than abandoning him to his fate and living happily with the man she truly loves. The development of the plot reveals a deepening of her love for Polyeucte so that she gradually converts a chaste duty to an impassioned will to embrace his religion and die with him.

Corneille's approach to tragicomedy is very different from that of Shakespeare or Beaumont and Fletcher. Dryden realized this and devoted the second section of his essay *Of Dramatick Poesie* to a discussion of the comparative strengths and weaknesses of French and English drama. The arguments of his opposed characters Lisideius and Neander on this subject pinpoint the differences and serve to draw our attention to the extent to which Corneille's tragicomedy fits the Guarinian definition. English tragicomedy exploits a mixture of tone, a contrast of tragic and comic material, and is in this sense closer to Guarini's formula than are Corneille's plays which avoid humour and instead contrast the opposed forces of passion and intellect, of love and duty. Corneille's economical plots are decried by Neander as indicating a narrowness of imagination, but in his rigorous observation of the unity of action the French dramatist is much closer to Guarini who insisted that every intrigue and character be indissolubly bound up with the central issue. As Lisideius puts it:

> But if he would have us to imagine that in exalting one character the rest of them are neglected, and that all of them have not some share or other in the action of the play, I desire him to produce any of Corneille's Tragedies, wherein every person (like so many servants in a well-governed family) has not some employment, and who is not necessary to the carrying on of the plot, or at least to your understanding it.
>
> (p. 69)

Neander's criticism of the lack of both variety and action in French tragicomedy is countered by Lisideius's assertion that:

> 'Tis a great mistake in us to believe that the French present no part of the action on the stage: every alteration or crossing of a

design, every newsprung passion, and turn of it, is a part of the action, and much of the noblest, except we conceive nothing to be action till the Players come to blows.

(p. 72)

This is much closer to *Il Pastor Fido* than anything by Shakespeare or Beaumont and Fletcher – with the telling exception of *The Tempest*. Vital to the operation of Guarinian tragicomedy is the conversion of the destructive or villainous characters at the end of the play. Corisca must repent, though we may find her change of heart abrupt and unmotivated. The dénouements of many Jacobean romances depend on even more arbitrary manipulation, as Lisideius points out: 'It shows little art in the conclusion of a Dramatick Poem, when they who have hinder'd the felicity during the Four Acts, desist from it in the Fifth without some powerful cause to take them off their design' (p. 73). Corneille, by contrast, may be said to improve on Guarini in centring the development of the action of his three great tragicomedies on a carefully prepared and well-motivated conversion of vengeance to pity.

Corneille's dramas, observing the classical five-act structure, are in all essentials very close to the formula outlined by Guarini in both the *Compendio* and *Il Pastor Fido*. He presents us at the start of each play with a pressing issue (the 'urgente cagione') and in the first act contrasts the rival claims of passion and reason, a variation on the Guarinian alternation of comic and tragic scenes. The intrigue develops in Acts II and III, the new material being germane to the fates of the central characters. The point of greatest danger is reached in Act IV and gives way to the surprising but credible dénouement of the final act. Corneille, like Guarini, presents us with 'the danger not the death' and though Polyeucte is killed, this is not seen as a tragedy but a life-enhancing martyrdom. Hence Corneille is concerned with heightening and yet tempering his emotional effects. His contemporary, Racine, had argued in his Preface to *Bérénice*:

There is no necessity for there to be blood and deaths in a tragedy. It is sufficient that the action be grand, the actors be heroic, that the passions be excited and that the whole resounds with that majestic sadness which creates all the pleasure of tragedy.

(p. 21)

It could be argued that Racine is talking here rather about tragicomedy than tragedy. In *Bérénice* the passions aroused by the parting of the central trio are tempered by the fact that none of them is killed. Corneille chooses more acutely to arouse the emotions of his audience as to the fate of his protagonists, all of whom are brought to the brink of death, but the 'tempering' results from their salvation at the last moment. This is identical with Guarini's technique in *Il Pastor Fido* and it serves the same overall aim: 'to purge with delight the melancholy of the audience' (*Compendio*, p. 246).

The tragicomedy of Corneille is a unique phenomenon. Racine came nearest to writing a drama in the mixed genre with *Mithridate* but his other plays are tragedies, concerned, like *Bérénice*, with dissolution. Molière's comedies are in a sense the obverse side of the coin in an age of reason. They expose the folly of humanity and a play like *Dom Juan* in its savage clash of contrasted tones is nearer to the satire of the Jacobeans than to the careful fusion of opposites effected by Corneille. Corneille's plays have not retained their popularity and are little read outside France although *Le Cid* has enjoyed a far greater success than any of his later dramas. This is perhaps significant. It is the least restrained of his plays, the most varied in character and action. It is the more vital because we feel the vastness of its scope even through its careful observation of the rules. It has not been the model for later dramas because after the *grand siècle* the ideal of a careful balance between intense passion and reason was outmoded. *Le Cid* represents the supreme flowering of neo-classical tragicomic romance. Nothing comparable was written in France until Victor Hugo produced *Hernani* in 1830 by which time tragicomedy was no longer regarded as a means of effecting dramatic synthesis.

PART II

The nineteenth and twentieth centuries: modern Romanticism and realism

5
Melodrama

> Lady Audley. Die! [*Pushes him down the well, the ruined stones fall with him.*] He is gone – gone! and no-one was a witness to the deed!
> Luke [*looking on, right upstage entrance*]. Except me!
>> (Colin Hazlewood, *Lady Audley's Secret*)

In the first half of our study we examined the neo-classical drama of the Renaissance and the seventeenth century. The growth of Romanticism in the late eighteenth and early nineteenth centuries had a pronounced effect on the form of drama generally and on the structure and development of tragicomedy in particular. We have seen in the satiric drama of the Jacobean period an exploitation of the clash between order and destruction, both in the content and the form of the plays, particularly in the drama of Marlowe. In *Doctor Faustus* the neat inevitability of the spiritual issues conflicting with the boundless aspiration of the Renaissance humanist finds an echo in the tragicomic structure of the play. Here medieval Morality and Miracle play forms are confronted by a Renaissance insistence on the complexity of ethical issues and an emphasis on secular traditions of comedy. Goethe's *Faust* reflects a parallel clash of ethical values and theatrical forms. This vast two-part drama, more completely tragicomic than Marlowe's play in its combination of serious and comic issues as well as in its more ambiguous ethical conclusions, is a confrontation of neo-classical and romantic values at the end of the eighteenth century. In his version of *Iphigenia* – an outstanding example of the neo-classicism of the age – Goethe had extended the tragicomic implications of the Euripides original in reworking a tragedy with a happy ending, a vital issue according to Guarini's commentary on Aristotle's *Poetics*. In addition, in such plays as *Götz Von Berlichen* he had already inaugurated the 'Sturm und Drang' movement which was to become the basis of eighteenth-century romantic drama's challenge to classicism.

The fight between neo-classical and romantic values was taken several stages further in France with Victor Hugo's onslaught on outmoded moral, social and theatrical beliefs in *Hernani*. Neither this play, nor Goethe's early dramas, nor the more significant contributions to the 'Sturm and Drang' movement such as Schiller's *Die Raüber* are tragicomedies. But they are important in one sense to our study in that they inevitably prepared the way for the most important popular threatrical genre of the nineteenth century, the one most influential in the later development of tragicomedy: melodrama. The larger-than-life figures of Hugo and Schiller, their extravagant attitudes and shocking ethics, may have seemed very modern at the time. Now they seem rather an exaggerated response to prevailing ideas. The world inhabited by their heroes and heroines is an essentially literary one and hence unreal. Melodrama developed inevitably from this romantic style of theatre. But it is also important to observe the further affinities between the popular melodrama of the nineteenth century and the equally escapist and unrealistic romances of the early Jacobean period. The basic mechanism which informs the working of a melodrama has much in common with that which animates a romantic tragicomedy; both can be profitably analysed with reference to Guarini's formulations. Even more important, melodrama is the key to understanding several of the seminal dramatists of the twentieth century. Both Shaw and Chekhov consciously refined melodrama structures and made them basic to their plays. In its final decadent flowering, the Grand Guignol, melodrama influenced Artaud whose Theatre of Cruelty is a savage modern version of the mixed genre.

We should begin, therefore, by examining the basic formula of popular melodrama and compare this both to the structure of

Jacobean romance and the example outlined by Guarini. Victorian melodrama, like Jacobean romance, is essentially an escapist idiom. Both are nearer to fairy-tale than real life, nearer to myth, to archetype. They share a common origin in folk culture. The characters are severely polarized into good and bad, black and white; the same key figures recur again and again. The evil agents are irredeemably wicked, wholly unsympathetic, for example Clion and Dionyza in *Pericles*, the Queen in *Cymbeline* (who like her counterpart in *Snow White* needs no name), Antonio in *The Tempest*, or the ranks of villains from Hatchet to Lady Audley. The virtuous heroine assumes an unusually important focus in this context. It is she rather than the hero who is at the centre of the drama and again she is an ideal rather than a reality. All the heroines in Shakespeare's romances have symbolic names: Marina, Imogen, Perdita and Miranda; the innocence of the Victorian damsel in distress is no less significant. All are victims who must suffer. Purity is their ultimate defence. It protects them all – from Marina and Miranda to Black-Ey'd Susan and Mary Wilson – from the worst threats of rape and murder. Their virtue is seen to have an almost supernatural force, but it is often assisted by the arbitrary intervention of a comic man. This figure takes various shapes: the Country Fellow who interrupts Philaster's assault on Arethusa, the clowns, Trinculo and Stephano, who serve to distract Caliban from his devilish plan, the genial Myles-na-Coppaleen, the more sinister Luke Marks.

Shakespeare is less preoccupied with a dramatic formula than Beaumont and Fletcher or the writers of popular Victorian melodrama. Shakespeare's great achievement in *The Tempest* is to make art hide art: we are unaware of the play's dramatic structure. This is not the case with the drama of Beaumont and Fletcher whose plots creak as surely as those of melodrama. All these writers of romantic theatre are creating tragicomedy in that they are concerned with a story of a suffering heroine at the centre of an intrigue which often results in the loss of home and loved ones; a heroine who is exposed to the dangers of rape and murder but is restored through a timely rescue to her family and former fortunes. Many of the features of Guarinian tragicomedy are evident here. The emotional effects are heightened as tragedy threatens, but tempered with the final escape. We are concerned with 'the danger, not the death'. Both the neo-classical tragicomedies and the nineteenth-century melodramas result in a happy ending which comes as a surprise. The plotting throughout is in accord with Guarini's 'ordine comico': it is more open, more clearly exposed to the audience. From the start there is a contrast in these dramas between tragedy and comedy. In the Jacobean romances this comes from the rich tradition of Elizabethan theatre, in the Victorian melodrama it arises from the ubiquitous nature and dominance of the comic man. When Luke Marks pops up to deliver the final line of the first act of *Lady Audley's Secret* we know villainy will be foiled. This does not detract from the element of suspense which is vital to both these versions of tragicomedy. Guarini's example of the 'leggiadra donna' – the loose woman who offers 'baits to desire' – as an image of the suspenseful plot is particularly appropriate here. What is more significant, however, is the credibility of the dénouement. This is not the strongest feature of the plays of Beaumont and Fletcher, nor – as Shaw was quick to point out (Preface, *Cymbeline Refinished*, pp. 133–8) – of Shakespeare's earlier romances. That the happy ending, however contrived, is always expected in popular melodrama is a tribute rather to the expectations of the audience. They accepted – demanded – a familiar pattern; it was vital to their emotional experience in the theatre. Guarini's aim – 'to purge with delight the melancholy of the audience' (*Compendio*, p. 246) – was never more accurately realized than by those Victorian dramatists who chose to exploit the emotional responses of their audience by a well-tried formula. The potential of melodrama to inflame the passions of an underpaid, overworked urban proletariat and thus arouse their sense of social injustice was realized only by those writers who chose to alter the components of this dramatic genre and in so doing radically change its tragicomic structure.

In his study of English melodrama Michael Booth says:

> Essentially melodrama is a dream world inhabited by dream
> people and dream justice, offering audiences the fulfilment and
> satisfaction found only in dreams. An idealization and simplifi-
> cation of the world of reality, it is in fact the world its audience
> want but cannot get. Melodrama is therefore a dramatization of
> this world, an allegory of human experience dramatically ordered,
> as it should be rather than it is.
>
> (*English Melodrama*, p. 14)

Though there is much truth in Booth's generalizations, a glimpse
at John Walker's *The Factory Lad* or Boucicault's *The Colleen
Bawn* indicates that it is far from the whole truth. Melodrama can
approach more closely to the dangers and problems of real life (as
in the serious handling of the political and social themes in the
former) or can present a far more complex picture of crime and
guilt (as in the characterization of the four 'villains' in the latter).
But even taking into account the above two plays – and such works
as Sedley's *The Drunkard* or Jerrold's *The Mutiny at the Nore*
which tackle unpleasant subjects in an uncompromising manner,
or Lewis's *The Bells* which is highly complex and original in its
approach to psychology and morality – the drama is far removed
from the conditions of the society who watched it. It is in essence
an escapist form, even – perhaps most pronouncedly – when
presenting hardship, poverty and crime. The early melodrama
theatres were situated either in the East End of London (like the
Britannia in Hoxton) or in more unsavoury areas south of the
Thames (like the Coberg – renamed the Royal Victoria – in the
New Cut). Dickens describes the audience at the Britannia in the
early years of Victoria's reign:

> Besides prowlers and idlers, we were mechanics, clock labourers,
> costermongers, petty tradesmen, small clerks, milliners, stay-
> makers, shoe-binders, slop workers, poor workers in a hundred

highways and byeways. Many of us – on the whole the majority
– were not at all clean, and not at all choice in our lives or conversation.

('Two views of a cheap theatre', *The Uncommercial
Traveller*, Oxford, 1958, p. 39)

We shall see from an examination of a cross-section of nineteenth-
century melodramas the potential of this tragicomic form to cater
for the emotional and imaginative needs of its highly volatile audience.

An important ingredient of melodrama which accounts for the
intensity of its appeal is music. The Licensing Act of 1837 forbade
all but two theatres – Drury Lane and Covent Garden (with the
addition later of the Theatre Royal in the Haymarket) – to put on
serious plays. The 'minor' theatres, restricted to spectacles and
musical pieces, soon learnt how to evade the law by including
music in dramatic works. The situation led to ludicrous abuses,
amusingly described by Jerome K. Jerome in *On the Stage and Off*:

Nearly all the performers had a bar of music to bring them on
each time, and another to take them off; a bar when they sat
down, and a bar when they got up again; while it took a small
overture to get them across the stage. As for the leading lady,
every mortal thing she did or said, from remarking that the snow
was cold in the first act, to fancying she saw her mother and then
dying in the last, was preceded by a regular concert.

(London, 1885, p. 39)

Nevertheless the genre could not have existed without it, not only
from a pragmatic point of view, but also from one of effectiveness.
Music, by heightening the excitement and pathos of the action,
helped the audience to suspend their disbelief and be drawn into
the world of romance. Shakespeare employed music, albeit more
sparingly, to this end, nowhere more effectively than in the
moments of reawakening and rebirth which represent the turning-
points in *Pericles*, *The Winter's Tale* and *The Tempest*. Music is a

most potent agent in softening the potentially painful emotional force of the events in melodramas. Crowded with incident as they are, and bristling with dangers to the lives of the protagonists, such dramas could not prepare the audience for the change of fortunes and the rescues which resolve the action without music. It gives the unreal and extreme events both charm and credibility.

Jerrold's *Black-Ey'd Susan* (1829) illustrates the basic features of melodrama, being very conventional in its emotional and ethical approach as well as clear-cut in its dramatic technique. The opening scene contrasts the villainy of the landlord Doggrass with the essential goodness of Gnatbrain whose comic function is taken further in the third scene when he is obliged to hide in a cupboard. Having been thus from the start accustomed to the mixture of the threatening and the comic, the audience are prepared to accept the fact that the eviction of Susan is prevented by Gnatbrain's discovery and further treatment of the bailiff, Jacob Twigg. Such complications of plotting as arise are made clear to the audience from the start as when we see Hatchet's false story of William's death at sea immediately following his payment of Susan's rent. With each act the danger to Susan and William increases, but throughout the audience have been given hints as to how tragedy will be avoided. Hatchet's threat to Susan is built into a big emotional scene in which the audience, fully aware of William's presence throughout, wait for the climax when the hero steps forward to confound the villain's plot. The capture of the smugglers at the end of Act I means that, after conveniently paying Susan's debt to Doggrass, Hatchet himself is arrested. Thus by the middle of Act II both financial and emotional dangers have been averted. It is necessary, therefore, at this point to introduce a new complication: the Captain's passion for Susan. Having announced 'I must and will possess her' he takes over the role of aggressor from Doggrass and Hatchet. Previously William has poured contempt on 'His Beelzebub's ship, the Law', which in the person of Doggrass has been seen to be a class enemy; now the Captain makes a more sinister antagonist whom William must attack physically.

Act III traces the consequences of this in William's trial and sentence as a series of highly emotive scenes – Willam's passionate defence of the assault, his sharing out of his few possessions and his last meeting with Susan, all underscored with music – bring the tragic implications to a climax. The timely and last-minute reversal is anticipated by the repeated thwarting of villainy earlier, the Captain's repentance when he is struck by William and Doggrass's previous confession to the audience of his receipt of the mysterious package.

This type of plotting is a cruder version of Guarini's insistence on the subtleties of intrigue which, he argues, are characteristic of the 'ordine comico'. The writers of melodrama – certainly in the early Victorian period – were dealing with a public whose education and consequent theatrical requirements were very different from those of the audiences in England or Italy at the beginning of the seventeenth century. This is particularly evident in the relishing of the – to our tastes – crude device of having William literally upstage Hatchet by appearing bang on cue: 'His shipmate turned round and saw . . .' (*Black-Ey'd Susan*, p. 22). Such a device was intended to be comic, not in the burlesque sense it now appears to us, but in that it undoubtedly encouraged a noisy response from an audience eager to join in the theatrical game. The same trick occurs later in another play, Hazlewood's *Lady Audley's Secret* (1863) where the potential for audience interjection and comic implication are pushed to their limit. Here the villainess exults in soliloquy, the openness of her cunning further complementing the timely entry and actions of the hero:

> *Lady Audley.* Once I was a fool to wed for love. Now I have married for wealth. What a change from the wife of George Talboys to the wife of Sir Michael Audley! My fool of a first husband thinks me dead. Oh excellent scheme, Oh cunning device! how well you have served me. [*George enters at back and comes down silently to her side.*] Where can he be now? Still in India no doubt. He is mourning my death, perhaps – ha, ha!

Why, I have only just begun to live – to taste the sweets of wealth and power. If I am dead to George Talboys, he is dead to me. Yes, I am well rid of him, and on this earth we meet no more.

George [*touching her on the shoulder*]. Yes, we do.

(*Nineteenth-Century Plays*, p. 245)

It is important for the eventual happy outcome of melodrama that, from the start, the wicked characters be more firmly circumscribed through devices which in their affinity with comedy mitigate the tragic implications of their actions.

The meeting between Lady Audley and her first husband culminates in her attempt on his life. As she brains him and then pushes his body down the well, her gloating final lines are countered by a cryptic remark from the wings, which she does not hear: it is the voice of the drunken gamekeeper Luke Marks, the comic man, who has seen and overheard her. Subsequently he will blackmail her and it is his interference which ensures that she is finally brought to justice. The figure of the comic man is vital in the workings of the melodrama plot: he has a signficance well beyond that so amusingly described by Jerome K. Jerome in *Stageland*:

He is very good is the comic man. He can't abear villainy. To thwart villainy is his life's ambition, and in this noble object fortune backs him up grandly. Bad people come and commit their murders and thefts right under his nose, so that he can denounce them in the last act.

They never see him there standing close beside them while they are performing these fearful crimes.

(pp. 21–2)

The comic man is another reincarnation of the Vice: a character who disturbs the smooth flow of the plot, interfering in the action to comic effect though with serious results. Nor is he a straightforwardly farcical figure of fun; Jerome adds: 'occasionally of late years, the comic man has been a bad man, but you can't hate him for it' (p. 25). Luke Marks is such a figure, threatening and sinister: he blackmails Lady Audley, ill-treats his wife and, after delivering his final indictment of the villainess, drops dead. Jerome K. Jerome emphasizes also that:

> He is a man of humble station, the comic man. The village blacksmith or a pedlar. You never see a rich or aristocratic comic man on the stage. You can have your choice on the stage; you can be funny and of lowly origin, or you can be well-to-do and without any sense of humour.
>
> (p. 21)

The comic man is vital in the manipulation of the audience's sympathies and his class is significant. In *The Drunkard* (1844) the hero, Edward Middleton, is saved from the consequences of his own alcoholism by his foster-brother, William, an innocent rustic whose semi-miraculous appearance on several occasions averts the danger into which the protagonists have fallen. When the heroine, Mary, is being threatened by the villain, Cribbs, with a fate worse than death, William appears out of nowhere to thwart him:

> *Cribbs.* Nay then, proud beauty, you shall know my power – 'tis late – you are unfriended, helpless, and thus – [*He seizes her.*]
> *Mary.* Help! Mercy! [*She struggles with Cribbs – William enters hastily, seizes Cribbs and throws him round, he falls.*]
> *William.* Well, squire, what's the lowest you'll take for your rotten carcase? Shall I turn auctioneer, and knock you down to the highest bidder? I don't know much of pernology, but I've a great notion of playing Yankee Doodle on your organ of rascality. Be off, you ugly varmint, or I'll come the steam engine, and set your paddles going all-fired quick.
>
> (*Victorian Melodramas*, p. 126)

It is William who also discovers Edward writhing with DTs in 'a wretched outhouse or shed near a tavern' and he who overhears Cribbs's plot to ruin him by forging his signature on a cheque.

In this figure, so central to the plotting of melodrama, the essential vitality of the genre is most clearly to be seen.

This is as true of the American stage as the English. *The Drunkard* is an American piece; for Boucicault also enjoyed great success there, while being the most prolific and skilful creator of melodrama in England. The part of Myles-na-Coppaleen, tailored to his own histrionic skills, is a more subtle variation on the stock character of the comic man than the crude archetype of William Dowton; and *The Colleen Bawn* (1860), the drama in which he occupies the central role, is a work of considerable originality and subtlety within the conventions of the genre. There is a pressing issue which initiates the plot: Hardress's need to marry the wealthy heiress, Anne Chute, in order to save himself and his mother from the threats of the 'pettifogging attorney', Corrigan. His secret marriage to the Colleen Bawn, Eily, makes this impossible and is the ground of all the complications that arise; these are in turn intensified through the scheming of Danny Mann who drops the incriminating letter from Hardress, thereby deceiving Anne into thinking that Kyrle Daly, the man she really loves, is unfaithful to her. These twists of plot are exploited in a sensational manner as befits the melodrama genre, notably when Anne mistakes the cloaked figure of Hardress for Kyrle and when she is later prevented from reading the marriage certificate by Danny's timely intervention. Danny's sudden appearances and interferences in the plot – as when he appears at the window and proceeds to inform Mrs Cregan of the fact that Hardress's glove is being used as a sign to remove Eily – give him some of the dramatic functions of the comic man; but he is in this respect contrasted with Myles who is at hand to undermine Danny's influence on the characters. The intrigue deepens through each of the three acts and requires an increasing ingenuity on Myles's part to thwart the villainy. Thus Act I ends with the powerful scene in which he prevents Hardress from destroying the wedding certificate, Act II culminates in his shooting of the villain (in mistake for an otter!) and spectacular rescue of the heroine; Act III needs his presence – and

his introduction of Eily – to turn the potentially tragic consequences into a double wedding.

The Colleen Bawn illustrates precisely to what extent melodrama
is a variation on the Guarini formula for tragicomedy. With all the
deception peculiar to comedy and the dangers appropriate to
tragedy, *Il Pastor Fido* is essentially a static play. If it is true – as
Philip Edwards argues – that *The Faithful Shepherdess* represents a
reworking of this 'in slow-motion tempo', nineteenth-century
melodrama by contrast speeds up the pace to an exaggerated
degree: it is rather like watching a film run at the wrong speed.
Jerrold, in contrasting melodrama with 'legitimate' drama
(tragedy and comedy), argued it was 'physical' in character as
distinct from 'mental': for him a melodrama is a piece 'with what
are called a great many telling situations' (*Stratford-upon-Avon
Studies*, I, p. 174). The author of the preparatory remarks to
Samuel Arnold's *The Woodman's Hut* (1814) gives us more idea of
the implications of this:

> If it [melodrama] err in having too much action, it has a counter-
> balancing advantage in not being clogged by excess of speech; in
> fact the music supplies the place of language . . . melodrama
> depends upon the strength of incident. It places characters in
> striking situations, leaving the situations to tell for themselves,
> and carefully avoids encumbering them with language.
>
> (Quoted in *English Melodrama*, pp. 38–9)

Boucicault does not fall into the same trap as Shakespeare in *Cymbeline*. Though the audience are fully prepared for the details of
the denouement – they have heard Danny's confession, they know
of Hardress's repentance and they have seen Eily safe in Myles's
hut – they are gripped by its unfolding. This is far from the redun-
dant *éclaircissement* that Shaw so objected to in *Cymbeline*, where
the characters do nothing but talk: here is an action-packed scene
with unexpected twists (such as Mrs Corrigan's confession) and a
series of powerful explosive theatrical entrances.

Boucicault's drama also tempers the danger to the characters through the dramatization of a contrasted group of schemers. Only Corrigan in the play could be classed as a typical melodrama villain and his threats — essentially financial — do not continue beyond the initial complication; his eavesdropping on Danny's confession comes to nothing and at the end of the play he is ignominiously ducked as he tries to creep away. Far more complex is Boucicault's presentation of Danny Mann and his relationship with the anti-hero, Hardress. Danny's servility goes well beyond the norm, owing a great deal to the source: both the true story and its adaptation in Gerald Griffin's novel *The Collegians* (1829). Boucicault's alterations to the story reveal precisely how he adapted an unsavoury crime to the requirements of melodrama, minimizing its offensiveness and translating a sordid sex murder not into tragedy but tragicomedy. The real facts of the case were very different, as Colin Wilson points out in *A Casebook of Murder*:

> For the modern reader the case of the Colleen Bawn ('white girl') is altogether less interesting than it was to the Victorians. They saw it as a moral tale of a wicked seducer, an innocent country girl and so on, forgetting that Ellie Hanley stole the life savings of the man who brought her up, and then spent most of it on clothes. She may have been injured, but she was not innocent. Scanlon [Hardress] himself certainly provides material for moralizing — spoilt, selfish and cowardly, without even the courage to commit his own murder. The most interesting person in the case is Sullivan [Danny Mann].
>
> (London, 1969, p. 107)

Sullivan was in fact Scanlon's ex-batman who offered to take the blame for seducing Ellie, was unable at first to kill her because she smiled at him, but finally murdered her in a sadistic frenzy. In adapting this to the stage Boucicault kept some of the complications of character but totally changed the outcome. In order that his audience should enjoy to the full the happy ending he replaced the outright wickedness of one man — tragic in its implications — with the scheming of three people, thus coming close to Guarini's tragicomic formulation. It is the business of Hardress's glove in the middle of the play which extends this aspect as the equivocations of the plotting renders all three – Hardress, Danny and Mrs Cregan – equally guilty. Significantly they must all repent, which they do spectacularly in the last act, and thus prepare the audience for the reconciliation which ensues.

Melodrama in general tends in fact towards a double outcome, like Miss Prism's 'three volume novel of more than usually revolting sentimentality' (*The Importance of Being Earnest*, London, 1966, p. 68) in which 'the good ended happily and the bad unhappily' (p. 28), with the additional implications of Oscar Wilde's ironic corollary: 'that is what fiction means' (p. 28). This formula is confirmed by a consideration of those dramas which are a clear exception to the general rule. Jerrold's *The Mutiny at the Nore* (1830), for instance, is very different from his conventional *Black-Ey'd Susan* and it is significant that this drama, also concerned with insubordination and the threat of execution, should both carry the events through to a tragic conclusion, and encourage the audience to expect this as clearly as they expect the reverse in *Black-Ey'd Susan*. The play, based on a historical event and character – Richard Parker – clearly offered a very different form of entertainment from the escapism common to the genre as the prefatory remarks make clear:

> Those who cannot conveniently attend a naval execution, may have their soft sympathies excited, and their curiosity gratified, by witnessing this drama. The paraphernalia of death is most correctly brought to view; and if to behold a picture of domestic agony, a frantic wife, and a poor unconscious infant in the stern grip of the executioners, be an added charm, the veriest amateur in such horrors will not be disappointed.
>
> (*The Mutiny at the Nore*, London, 1830, p. 8)

The way the drama develops towards its tragic climax precisely avoids the techniques employed in a play like *The Colleen Bawn*: there is no humour, no complexity of intrigue, and, more significantly, no comic man. Parker describes the injuries he has undergone in the navy in such a graphic, emotional way that there is no possibility of this story of revenge having any outcome but a profoundly unhappy one. The same thing is true of *The Factory Lad*, performed at the Surrey Theatre, the home of nautical melodrama from the 1820s onwards. This play similarly pursues an inexorable course in narrating the actions of a group of machine-breakers who set fire to the factory of their heartless young employer; when finally brought to court and sentenced, the leader Rushton 'laughing hysterically' shoots the owner. Both these plays were exploiting to the full the horrific aspects of melodrama, and whether or not we see the aim of the dramatists as extending the emotionally subversive potential of the class conflicts basic to the genre, there is no doubt that their skills were employed to very different ends from those we have examined elsewhere in the chapter.

In the case of Lewis's *The Bells* (1871) the manipulation of the features peculiar to this dramatic genre is productive of something even further removed from tragicomedy. Lewis's play was written for a very different audience from that which attended the Surrey or Britannia theatres; he was writing for a West End audience and providing Irving – as it transpired – with one of his greatest successes. The character of Matthias is one of the most complex in the range of English melodrama and far more sympathetic than his counterpart in Lewis's source, Erckmann-Chatrian's *The Polish Jew*. His heroic stature is emphasized by the way in which Lewis handles the plot. This drama is remarkable for its restrained treatment of violence. The horror is no less intense because the terrors are in Matthias's mind, however; indeed they take on the quality of nightmare which through its relentlessness fully prepares the audience for the final agonizing death of the protagonist: the Burgomaster staggers out of his room with the words: 'Take the rope from my neck'. This is the only point at which the violence is visible on stage and was an addition of Irving's: in *The Polish Jew* he dies off stage. Here we have a deliberate negation of the most basic aspect of the genre. There is precisely no plot against

Matthias: he himself instigates his own trial and destruction. The dramatic conflict is internalized and the more overt physical confrontations which characterize the genre are consequently confounded, the result being far more emotionally disturbing. It is deeply significant that Matthias should assure us − and himself − 'Not like that, not like that am *I* to be caught' (p. 486) when Sozel shows him the account of the robbers whose crime came to light twenty-three years later through the discovery of the blade of an old knife. Lewis, as surely as his hero, scorns such devices and in so doing turns his back on the conventions fundamental to melodrama. In so doing he creates a drama which is much closer to tragedy than tragicomedy.

The Bells is significant in the development of melodrama for another, quite different, reason. It is a play particularly concerned with an extreme of emotional response: terror, and it strongly anticipates the final decadent flowering of the genre at the end of the century in Grand Guignol. *The Bells*, like many popular English melodramas, was based on a French original. It was the French who were to extend the implications of the melodrama genre into the Grand Guignol, itself an extreme example of the mixed theatrical mode. In 1896 Oscar Méténier opened his Grand Guignol theatre. Under the influence of Antoine and the Théâtre Libre he developed a type of entertainment which specialized in *moeurs populaires* and *faits divers*, short plays capitalizing on sensational events with the object of shocking. Under his successor, Max Maurey, the Grand Guignol shifted its emphasis to horror plays, alternating these with short farces to add piquancy in what were termed *douches écossaises* (hot and cold showers). This style of theatrical entertainment, which came into vogue in England at the beginning of this century, represents a savage variation on the formula of melodrama with its juxtaposition of comedy and tragedy. In extending these two contrasted elements into their respective extremes of the farce and the horror play, Grand Guignol was a means of exploiting to the full the audience's emotional responses. Antonin Artaud was to base his Theatre of Cruelty on this technique. He makes an intriguing contrast with two other writers who at the turn of the century were to take the basic formula of melodrama and shape it to their own very different ends: Chekhov and Shaw. In the dramas of these three key writers, concerned respectively with an emotional, a psychological and a social emphasis, we may observe the transformation of the melodrama genre into three contrasted and seminal variations of modern tragicomedy.

6
Variations of melodrama: Chekhov and Shaw

> *The Devil.* This marvellous force of Life of which you boast is a force
> of Death: Man measures his strength by his destructiveness. . . .
> It is the same in everything. The highest form of literature is the
> tragedy, a play in which everybody is murdered at the end.
> (Bernard Shaw, Man and Superman)

When the American director Joshua Logan visited Stanislavski in
Russia in the winter of 1930–1 he expressed surprise at the way in
which the plays of Chekhov were performed at the Moscow Art
Theatre:

> In the weeks and months that followed, we saw many plays
> directed by Stanislavski including *The Cherry Orchard* with
> Mme Chekhova in the leading role and the part originated by
> Stanislavski now being played by Kacholov. This, of course,
> was true Stanislavski – moody, thoughtful, and emotional. But
> it had an underlying earthy humor which was another surprize
> to us. There were often lusty physical jokes. I can remember
> Moskvin as Epikhodov watching the departing family talking
> while he nailed together some crates, his attention so fixed on
> the touching scene that he was constantly hitting his finger
> instead of the nail. All through Stanislavski's work there was a
> strong sense of humour, and it was boldly stated.
> (Foreword to S. Moore, The Stanislavski System,
London, 1966, pp. xiii–xiv)

Logan's comments are salutary, since there is still a tendency, particularly in England, to believe that the proper mood in Chekhov's

drama cannot be sustained unless the comic effects are severely muted. English critics were very ill at ease with both Paul Scho-field's Vanya (directed by Antony Page) in 1970 and John Wood's Ivanov (directed by David Jones) in 1976 because of the more extreme comic techniques tending in both cases towards farce. Moreover, when Logan saw his company, Stanislavski's work was very different from what it had been more than thirty years before when he originally performed the Chekhov plays. Then dramatist and director had had, from the start, radically different approaches to the plays as a glance at Stanislavski's prompt book for *The Seagull* reveals: he saw it as a naturalistic emotive *drama*, not essentially as a *comedy* (which was Chekhov's definition). When working on his last play *The Cherry Orchard* Chekhov, on 7 March 1901, wrote to Olga Knipper: 'the next play I write for the Art Theatre will definitely be funny, very funny – at least in intention' (*Chekhov: Letters*, New York, 1966, pp. 157–63), a comment Robert Brustein interprets as 'a sally aimed at Stanislavski' (*The Theatre of Revolt*, p. 167). He deplored the director's tendency to encourage his actors to emphasize the emotional life of his charac-ters and though Stanislavski did present *The Cherry Orchard*, as many directors after him have done, as a sombre study in Russian gloom, Chekhov insisted on calling it 'not a drama, but a comedy, in places almost a farce' (Letter to Maria Lilina, 15 September 1903, op. cit., pp. 157–63).

This dichotomy is particularly significant in an assessment of the tragicomic potential of Chekhov's plays. His mingling of con-trasted dramatic effects was to achieve a more complex fusion as he refined his theatrical techniques over the seventeen years which separate *Ivanov* (1887) and *The Cherry Orchard* (1904). The increasing subtlety of his method reveals a successful attempt to realize the full tragicomic potential of melodrama. In the growing depth of his characterization, in the careful plotting of his work (an art which more and more cunningly was to conceal art), and in his employment of comic effects to enrich the humanity of his scenes he brings to a height the dramatic form first given clear shape by

Guarini. It is consequently misleading to underemphasize or underplay the comedy in his work since then the careful balance of theatrical effects is disturbed. Particularly dangerous is the tendency to perform his plays as though through an imaginary 'fourth-wall' separating the audience from the stage. The psychological complexity and truth of Chekhov's mature plays too often leads actors into too introspective an approach whereas the techniques appropriate to comedy (with its firmer emphasis on the relationship between actor and audience) are as important as the in-depth naturalistic attitude to characterization. Ironically, Stanislavski is to blame for this since it was his production of *The Seagull* in 1898 which turned the disastrous reception of the première two years earlier in St Petersburg into a triumph which set the seal both on Chekhov's success and the theatrical approach which was henceforth to characterize productions of his work. Elsewhere – in his autobiography – Joshua Logan expresses even more marked surprise at Stanislavski's dismissal (in 1930) of precisely those emotional exercises which were to become basic to the American interpretation of his method; clearly Stanislavski had learnt much since he had first directed *The Seagull*.

The account of the Moscow première by Nemirovitch-Dantchenko, Stanislavski's collaborator, confirms the dramatic emphasis of this production:

> Life unfolded in such frank simplicity that the auditors seemed almost embarrassed to be present; it was as if they eavesdropped behind a door or peeped through a window. As you know there is no heroism of any kind in the play, no stormy theatrical experiences, no lurid spots to invoke sympathy, such spots as usually serve the actor to display his talents. Here was nothing but shattered illusions, and tender feelings crushed by contact with rude reality.
>
> (*My Life in the Russian Theatre*, London, 1968, p. 188)

The success of this interpretation was achieved at the expense of a more complex interplay of comic and tragic features which are

present from the start. The opening conversation instantly cap-
tures the ironic note which is basic to the play:

> *Medviedenko.* Why do you always wear black?
> *Masha.* I am in mourning for my life. I'm unhappy.
>
> (*The Seagull*, p. 119)

The performance of Konstantin's play in the first act – a play
within a play – offers (as that dramatic device always does) ample
opportunity for ironic distanced effects in the mixture of cruelty
and humour in the (stage) audience's response to it. The rows
between mother and son, both during the performance of his play
and later, expose the vanity and blindness of both in a rich comic
vein, notably in this confrontation:

> *Trepliov.* I refuse to accept you at your own valuation! I refuse to
> accept you or him!
> *Arkadina.* You're decadent!
> *Trepliov.* Take yourself off to your lovely theatre and go on act-
> ing in your futile, miserable plays!
> *Arkadina.* I've never acted in futile, miserable plays! Let me
> alone! You're incapable of writing even a couple of miserable
> scenes! You're just a little upstart from Kiev! A cadger!
> *Trepliov.* You miser!
> *Arkadina.* You beggar! Nonentity!
>
> (p. 159)

Significantly Arkadina's last two exclamations are separated by the
stage direction 'Treplev sits down and weeps quietly' (p. 159). His
mother immediately switches to an effusion of sympathy as intense
as her insults and with this Chekhov makes a sharp adjustment of the
tone of the scene. It is important for actors and audience to realize
both extremes; they complement one another not only in being
related to the artistic temperament of the two characters but also in
creating the mixed mood of the drama. The further implications

of Chekhov's irony are revealed later for in so far as the play is a comedy it is a savage one. By the end Nina has been destroyed by Trigorin (just like the seagull of the title) while we see Arkadina and her lover for the selfish creatures they both are. The marriage of Medviedenko and Masha is confirmed as the squalid compromise threatened earlier, and the play ends with Konstantin's suicide.

As Chekhov's theatricals skills developed he was to evolve a more and more subtle blend of dramatic contrasts. *The Seagull*, like its two predecessors *Ivanov* and *The Wood Demon*, involves the suicide of the central character: all three shoot themselves. In his later plays Chekhov carefully minimizes the tragic consequences by a concern for 'the danger, not the death'. Thus in *Uncle Vania* the protagonist, unlike his prototype in *The Wood Demon*, does not shoot himself: he attempts unsuccessfully to shoot someone else. In *The Three Sisters* there is a death, of the Baron in his duel with Toozenbach, but it is not at the centre of the action, being one of many contrasted strands of the complex dénouement. In his final play, *The Cherry Orchard*, no one is wounded or killed, not a single shot is fired. Gradually Chekhov converted the action and incident peculiar to melodrama into a more static form capable of sustaining a more reflective tone with constantly shifting moods. That the plays are in essence melodramas is stressed by Brustein who points to the fact that all Chekhov's mature works, most notably *The Cherry Orchard*, are constructed on the same melodrama pattern of 'the conflict between a despoiler and his victims' (*The Theatre of Revolt*, pp. 151–2), while the action follows the same development of 'the gradual dispossession of the victims from their rightful inheritance' (p. 152). In *The Seagull* Trigorin ruins Nina as Arkadina spiritually dispossesses Trepliov; in *Uncle Vania* Hélène steals Sonia's secret love while Serebriakov steals her inheritance; in *The Three Sisters* Natasha gradually evicts the Prozorov family; in *The Cherry Orchard* Lopakhin literally dispossesses Ranyevskaia and Gayev. The related symbols – of the seagull, the forests (in both *The Wood Demon* and *Uncle Vania*), the Prozorov home and the cherry orchard – serve to emphasize this. Brustein adds:

What prevents us from seeing these melodramatic configurations is the extraordinary way in which they have been concealed. Technically Chekhov's most effective masking device is to bury the plot so that violent acts and emotional climaxes occur offstage or between the acts. In this way he manages to avoid the melodramatic crisis and to obscure the external conflict, ducking the event and concentrating on the dénouement. Secondly, Chekhov concludes the action before the conventional melodramatic reversal: the triumphant victory of virtue over vice; in its place he substitutes a reversal of his own invention in which the defeated characters, shuffling off the old life, begin to look forward to the new. Most important, however, he refuses to cast his characters in conventional hero-villain roles. In the buried plot, Chekhov's despoilers act while his victims suffer; but by subordinating plot to character, Chekhov diverts our attention from process to motive and makes us suspend our judgment of the action.

(pp. 152–3)

The implication of Chekhov's theatrical development for the actor is seen in two revealing comments by John Gielgud (who played Trepliov in 1925 and Trigorin in 1936):

The Seagull is written in a more conventional manner than *The Cherry Orchard*. There are big acting scenes in every act and the four principal characters carry the interest in a far simpler method of exposition than in the later Chekhov plays. . . . *The Seagull* seemed to me a more conventional kind of play and I felt I understood it a little better, at least as regards the melodramatic side of the plot (the jealousies, quarrelling and Konstantin's suicide at the end).

(*Stage Directions*, London, 1979, p. 86)

The skills of a director have always been necessary to bring out and control the complex effects in Chekhov's plays, nowhere more so than in *The Cherry Orchard*. While being his most ruthless (in that the characters are completely robbed of their home and way of life), it is also – as he insisted – his most comic drama. The play does not end with an affirmation but with Feers's entrance and, as he curls up to die, we hear the orchard being put to the axe. Throughout, the tone of the play is ambiguous and our attitude to the characters is conditioned by Chekhov's more ironic approach. Madame Ranyevskaia is foolish and vain, Gayev little less so. In many ways they deserve to lose their home. The play has been seen as prophetic of the Russian Revolution and Chekhov's attitude to his indolent but fascinating and fully-drawn characters is indicative of his social and political as well as his human concerns. No mood is simple enough to establish itself for long. When Trofimov, the eternal student, argues justly with Madame Ranyevskaia in Act III he storms off and there is a sound of someone running quickly downstairs and suddenly falling with a crash. 'There are shrieks from Ania and Varia, followed by laughter' and 'Ania runs in laughing' to announce 'Pyetia's fallen downstairs' (p. 377). At the end of Act IV there is one of those scenes of unrequited love from which the playwright is able to extract such a variety of emotional responses. Varia's love for Lopakhin is returned, but he finds it impossible to propose to her. Finally the two are left together, prompted by Madame Ranyevskaia, but it is no use: he talks about his proposed journey and the weather, only too glad to make his excuses and go when he hears someone shout his name. The scene is richly comic in its observation of two embarrassed, tongue-tied characters, but tragic in its outcome as Varia is left in tears. The sustaining of a bitter-sweet mood is completely realized in this play, notably in the second act in which the action is minimal and the various strands of conversation are orchestrated with off-stage voices, the melancholy song on Yepihodov's guitar and the unusual noise 'as if out of the sky, like the sound of a string snapping, slowly and sadly dying away' (p. 365). As Nemirovitch-Danchenko puts it: 'The absurd and the pathetic, the noble and the worthless, the intelligent and the stupid, all are interwoven and assume a form of peculiar theatrical resonance becoming a harmony of human voices and external sounds' (*My Life in the Russian Theatre*, London, 1968, pp. 207–8).

Exactly how Chekhov came to achieve this extension of melodrama into a more subtle variation of tragicomedy is best observed by a consideration of how he perfected his theatrical technique in adapting an early play, *The Wood Demon*, to create *Uncle Vania*. In the former at the end of the second act occurs the baldest confrontation of contrasted feelings:

> *Elena Andreyevna.* There's no happiness for me in this world. No! . . . Why do you laugh?
> *Sonya* [*laughing and covering her face*]. I am so happy! So very happy!
> *Elena Andreyevna* [*wringing her hands*]. Indeed, how unhappy I am!

> (*The Wood Demon*, p. 139)

This is tragicomedy in the raw: there is a crude clash of opposites. By the time we reach this point in *Uncle Vania* not only does Chekhov omit Hélène's response to Sonia's outburst, but the latter's joy is tempered by the far more complex series of circumstances which have led up to this scene. Astrov (the Krouschov character) does not return Sonia's love and thus at this point in the drama she is puzzled by her own happiness; Hélène's praise of Astrov thrills her but she experiences too the hopelessness of loving him. She expresses her true feelings for him only sub-textually, notably when Chekhov reworks Voynitsky's ironic speech on the forests by giving it to her as an indirect expression of her admiration for Astrov. A darker note is more subtly introduced in the scene between Sonia and Astrov by his confession that Hélène might turn his head and by his reference to the patient who died under chloroform, an incident (new to this play) which he has described at length in the first act. Chekhov has also cut three major characters from the earlier play so as to concentrate more fully on the complexities of relationships within a smaller group. In Act III he introduces new twists in the plotting which prepare us for the comedy of Vania's bungled murder attempt which ends the act. The new plotting also enriches the emotional complexities of the action. When Vania leaves to fetch the roses Sonia confesses her love of Astrov to Hélène, who offers to help. But instead, her attempts lead to Astrov's proposal to her, to her responding by letting him kiss her and to the consternation – serious in its outcome but farcical in its presentation – of Vania's perfectly mistimed entrance. The complexity of the resultant situation enriches the tragicomic potential of Serebriakov's announcement of his plan to sell the estate. This culminates in the fusion of the dangerous, the pathetic and the ludicrous in Vania's conduct:

> *Voinitsky.* Let me go, Hélène! Let me go! [*Freeing himself from her, runs in and looks round for Serebriakov.*] Where is he? Ah, there he is! [*Fires at him.*] Bang! [*A pause*] Missed? Missed again! [*Furiously*] Damnation! . . . devil . . . devil take it! [*Flings the revolver on the floor and sinks on to a chair, exhausted.*]

(Uncle Vania, p. 233)

Act III of *The Wood Demon* ends in the bleakest tragedy, with Voynitsky's suicide and Elena's desperate plea to escape. This gives way to the unanimously happy resolution of Act IV in which all are forgiven and the lovers paired off. The perfunctory quality of this, the crudest of melodramatic reversals which is very difficult to bring off on stage, is replaced in *Uncle Vania* by a new type of dénouement in which, by extending the mixture of dramatic forms established earlier, Chekhov makes an original contribution to the genre of tragicomedy. The act is in effect a prolonged leave taking such as recurs in *The Three Sisters* and *The Cherry Orchard*. An elegiac note is struck from the start in the conversation of Telyeghin and Marina and throughout the action Chekhov gives his playwriting pronounced musical affinities, with the quiet accompaniment provided by Telyeghin's guitar playing and in the emphatic patterning of the language, notably the phrase 'They've gone' which is repeated towards the end with increasing lyrical force. In this act the characters do not – as in the earlier version of the story – suddenly and unconvincingly change; there are no dramatic conversions. Astrov still wants Hélène to keep her appointment with him; while Serebriakov perfunctorily forgives Vania, having been quite unaffected by the attempt on his life. Even Vania's thoughts of suicide are realistically defeated by the conduct of Sonia and Astrov. All are obliged to face the consequences of their own actions and those of others. The play ends with Sonia's tearful comforting of Vania. This has a parallel with the last scene of *The Three Sisters*. It also bears out the truth of Edward Bond's defence of a similar dogged determination in the face of defeat in his play *Saved*:

> If the spectator thinks this is pessimistic that is because he has not learned to clutch at straws. Clutching at straws is the only realistic thing to do. The alternative, apart from the self-indulgence of pessimism, is a fatuous optimism based on superficiality of both feeling and observation.
>
> (p. 5)

There are strong parallels between Chekhov's last play and Shaw's *Heartbreak House*. This 'fantasia in the Russian manner on English themes' is concerned, as Shaw put it, with 'the same nice people, the same utter futility' (p. 4). Chekhov, he argues, 'had no faith in these charming people extricating themselves. They would, he thought, be sold up and sent adrift by the bailiffs; therefore he had no scruple in exploiting and even flattering their charm' (p. 3). Shaw does exactly the same thing with the Shotover household and its guests in order to portray his disillusioned picture of a morally and politically vacuous society hastening to destruction on the eve of the First World War. His theatrical technique – notably in the final act – owes much to Chekhov, particularly to the second act of *The Cherry Orchard*, as Margery M. Morgan has pointed out:

> In both the suspension of dramatic action reflects the arrested life of a society about to break up and from its ruin perhaps

release the germ of a new order. The ensemble nature of both
plays is evident in the grouping of figures in these analogous
scenes: no single one dominant as they sit or lie, or aimlessly
wander about the stage.

(The Shavian Playground, p. 209)

She draws attention to Randall's flute playing in place of Yepihodov's strumming on the mandolin, the feeling of presentiment
in Hector and Firs, and the strange interruption of the Shavian
burglar which matches the equally odd and disturbing entrance of
the tramp in the Chekhov play. What such a comparison fails to
emphasize, however, is that Shaw was influenced here to a fault.
The Chekhovian mood piece was as alien to him as the pessimism
he temporarily embraced in this atypical drama with its shift of
mood from the farcical to the gloomy. That historical circumstances had led to this is made clear in the lengthy preface which
also points out why such a play had to wait until after the war to be
performed. Shaw loses nothing of his wit in this work and employs
it to sharpen his satiric portrait of this doomed civilization, but in
the context of his drama as a whole the Chekhovian note he sounds
here has an uncharacteristic and false ring.

Shaw's contribution to tragicomedy, though it too emerged from
a careful manipulation of melodrama, owes far more to Ibsen than
to Chekhov. Ibsen had revealed to Shaw the potential of tragicomedy in being a more cruel and disturbing dramatic form than
either tragedy or comedy. Of a performance of *The Wild Duck* he
exclaimed:

> To sit there getting deeper and deeper into that Ekdal home, and
> getting deeper and deeper into your own life all the time, until
> you forget that you are in a theatre at all; to look on with horror
> and pity at a profound tragedy, shaking with laughter all the
> time at an irresistible comedy; not from a diversion, but from an
> experience deeper than real life ever brings to most men, or
> often brings to any man.

(Shaw, Our Theatre in the Nineties, III, p. 138)

As Shaw's dramatic skills developed he was to incline more and more firmly towards the comic rather than the tragic. His experience as a London theatre critic during the 1890s had made him profoundly contemptuous of the dramatic extremes which were popular on the contemporary stage. The social comedy of manners and the musical farce on the one hand were as repellent to him as serious drama on the other: the former was too trivial to be worthy of consideration, the latter, which he variously stigmatized with the terms 'sham Ibsenism', 'Sardoudeldom' and 'bardolatry', too romantic. Throughout his career Shaw firmly rejected tragedy as unworthy; he was too much of an optimist to embrace despair and too much of a realist to accept the clichés of the conventional theatre. His contempt for Pinero's *The Second Mrs Tanqueray* is revealing:

> The moment the point is reached at which the comparatively common gift of 'an eye for a character' has to be supplemented by the higher dramatic gift of sympathy with character − of the power of seeing the world from the point of view of others instead of merely describing them or judging them from one's own point of view in terms of the conventional system of morals, Mr Pinero breaks down.

> *(Our Theatre in the Nineties*, I, pp. 46−7)

It is the moment in Act III when Paula refuses to defend her strength of character as well as the end of the play when she conveniently goes off and commits suicide which Shaw considered mere palliatives to the audience's requirements and thus an abnegation of the dramatist's duty.

'I deal', he argued in the preface to *Major Barbara*, 'in the tragicomic irony of the conflict between real life and the romantic imagination' (p. 203): a statement applicable to his drama as a whole. We can most clearly see the distinction between his concept of comedy and tragicomedy by an examination of the dénouement of *Pygmalion*. This is one of his most immediately attractive (and popular) works, dealing as it does with an essentially romantic myth, itself analogous to the more familiar fairy-tales of the Ugly Duckling and Cinderella. Shaw handles social and political themes with an effective lightness of touch which in no way diminishes their force and carries the issues through right to the end. It is the confrontation of romance and reality which makes the final scene between Higgins and Eliza so complex in theatrical effect. One need not go as far as Allan J. Lerner who justified his adaptation (with Frederick Loewe), *My Fair Lady*, by arguing 'I have omitted the sequel (Shaw's epilogue) because in it Shaw explains how Eliza ends not with Higgins but with Freddy and – Shaw and Heaven forgive me – I am not certain he is right' (*My Fair Lady*, Harmondsworth, 1959, p. 6), to realize that the dénouement pulls us powerfully in different directions. Emotionally one feels for Eliza and because she and Higgins share a depth of understanding, one wills the two together, while at the same time recognizing intellectually that they would be incompatible as man and wife and that Eliza's decision is right. There can be no question of the play ending tragically, nor does Eliza, like the enlightened Marchbanks, rush out into the night, but beneath her pragmatic attitude and Higgins's coolly assured nonchalance there is a powerful sub-text of emotion which has built up from the previous acts and which functions here to qualify our acceptance of the neat resolution.

Shaw took pains to deflate, in his epilogue, the sentimental demand for the marriage of the two protagonists; he argues that the play *does* have a conventional ending (Eliza marries Freddy), but it is not the ending which the audience has been led to expect. This technique – of frustrating expectations – functions far more savagely in *Mrs Warren's Profession*. Shaw refuses to have his central character either conveniently kill herself (like Paula Tanqueray) or repent and change her way of life. Hence he avoids either tragedy or comedy, the more emphatically so as the young heroine, Vivie, does not marry Frank but, as the curtain falls, settles down to her work, happily absorbed in it, having just cheerfully torn up his note. Shaw classed this work as 'unpleasant' in his first volume of plays and he was well aware of its potential – in the manner of Ibsen – to disturb his audience. In this drama we can observe most clearly what he defined as the 'technical novelty in Ibsen's plays' which was to prove so influential both for him and for the new theatre movement in England:

> Formerly you had in what was called a well-made play an exposition in the first act, a situation in the second, an unravelling in the third. Now you have exposition, situation and discussion; and the discussion is the test of the playwright.
>
> (Shaw, *The Quintessence of Ibsenism*, p. 87)

The scene which ends *Mrs Warren's Profession* owes a great deal to the closing scene of *A Doll's House* but it takes the audience even more firmly off its guard because of the more extensive vein of comedy Shaw has explored throughout the play, and because it precisely reverses the more acceptable balance established in the parallel scene at the end of Act II. This earlier scene, in which Vivie faces her mother Mrs Warren, who powerfully defends herself, cunningly adapts many of the melodramatic devices employed elsewhere. They are observable in the stage directions which accompany the speeches of Mrs Warren: 'violently', 'raising her voice angrily', 'piteously', 'distractedly throwing herself on her knees' – directions which are in marked contrast to those for Vivie: 'quite unmoved', 'looking across at her without raising her head from her book', 'determinedly'. It is as though the very style of melodrama were being brought face to face with reason and argument. Significantly, in this scene the passionate feelings win through as Vivie, going from 'now thoughtfully attentive' to being 'more and more deeply moved', ends 'fascinated, gazing at her' and saying: 'My dear mother: you are a wonderful woman: you are stronger than all England' (*Mrs Warren's Profession*, p. 213). Shaw knows his audience must experience and feel the emotional strength of his ideas before he can drive home the critical intellectual issues: the audience shares Vivie's concern when she adds 'I believe it is I who will not be able to sleep now' (p. 213). But Shaw refuses to let his audience off the hook. Mrs Warren does not follow conventional stage precedents and, because she will not change her way of life now she is independent of her profession, Vivie proves even more remorseless in the final scene. Here her mother pulls out every emotional stop, not a single melodramatic effect remains unexploited, but her daughter – with Shaw – remains adamant. Hence Mrs Warren's gestures now seem empty and we are thus forced to probe beyond the characters to a clear awareness of the social, political and economic bases of Shaw's theme.

Other features, of plot and characterization, are drawn from the melodrama genre: notably the presentation of the villain, Sir George Crofts – a more sinister version of the predatory landlord – and the way in which his threatening conduct towards the heroine is foiled by the interruption of Frank, shot-gun in hand, in the role of the comic man. Such techniques are more fully exploited in *The Devil's Disciple*, as Shaw openly admitted:

> Every old patron of the Adelphi pit would, were he not beglamoured in a way presently to be explained, recognize the reading of the will, the oppressed orphan finding a protector, the arrest, the heroic sacrifice, the court martial, the scaffold, the reprieve at the last moment, as he recognizes beefsteak pudding on the bill of fare at his restaurant.
>
> (Preface, *Three Plays for Puritans*, p. xxii)

These melodramatic devices are carried right through to the end without a Shavian discussion to replace the unravelling; but in this drama the conventions are turned on their head in order to further the irony of the playwright's thesis. This centres on the paradox, finally explained in the denouement, that the Devil's Disciple, Dick, has found his true vocation as a preacher; the Minister, Anderson, has found his as a soldier. Both have seemed unheroic until this point; now their conduct is vindicated as Dick faces a martyr's death and Anderson successfully fights for a political cause. These 'diabolonian ethics' (as Shaw calls them in the preface) owe a great deal to the techniques of Bunyan and Blake; they are characteristic of all his mature dramas, and are given most forceful theatrical expression in *Major Barbara*. Shaw sees villainy thwarted but since this comprises on the one hand Swindon's defeat and on the other Mrs Dudgeon's death, he presents a neat reversal of accepted morals and ethics. In this work Shaw burlesques melodrama in order to question fundamental Victorian values and in so doing he turns to fresh use the tragicomic features of the genre.

In *Man and Superman* (1901–3) Shaw goes much further in his integration of comic and serious drama. In this instance a witty social comedy tending towards melodrama – in the flight, the ambush and the banditti – turns into the finest example of the dramatist's exploration of a theatre of pure thought. Here, however, the discussion occurs not at the end of the play, but in the middle. The transformation is achieved through musical effects, Wagnerian in inspiration, specifically Mozartian in application as the 'darkness deepens . . . and the sky seems to steal away out of the universe. Instead of the Sierra there is nothing' (*Man and Superman*, p. 83). This daring shift of mood is also achieved through the links between the Don Giovanni story in the outer plot and the four characters here – a soprano (Anna), a tenor (Juan), a 'nasal operatic baritone' (the Devil) and a comic basso (the Statue) – who take up the major theme of the work and develop it in the manner of a musical quartet. Central to the debate here is the dichotomy in Shaw's description of 'the Life Force', alternatively seen to be irresistible, impervious to logic and morals and yet a conscious extension of the human will, urging mankind to know, choose and understand his destiny. The middle section, a play within a play, ends with Anna's cry: 'I believe in the life to come. A father! A father for the Superman!' (p. 137): a cry which is to recur in *Major Barbara*. In both plays Shaw indicates the way forward not (as he will later in *Back to Methuselah*) by dramatizing this reality on stage, but by the hope vested in a marriage of opposites. In *Man and Superman* he marries the impractical philosophic idealist (Tanner) to the intuitive, contriving female intelligence (Anne). Tanner is in a sense the sacrificial victim, a stage in the development of the species like Wagner's Wotan who must make way for Siegfried. The philosophic themes explored in depth in the central section of the play are thus resolved in the comic dénouement of the outer section, for Shaw has created here an original dramatic structure enabling him – notably through arguments he puts in the Devil's mouth – to plumb the depth of a negative, tragic view of humanity, which he can subsequently confound in Juan's counter-arguments: a situation which anticipates the metamorphosis of his dangerous adversary into the comic villain, Mendoza.

Major Barbara is the richest and most complex of Shaw's plays. Again, this drama refuses to fit into a neat category as the final act relentlessly works out the implications of the previous confrontations of idealism and reality. At the end of Act II Barbara is in despair as her father, having kept his part of their bargain and visited her Salvation Army shelter, has successfully destroyed her faith and marches off triumphant with Cousins to the ironic accompaniment of 'Immenso giubilo'. Later Barbara's disillusionment will be seen as 'a tinpot little tragedy', as Andrew expounds Shavian morality: 'That is what is wrong with the world at present. It scraps its obsolete steam engines and dynamoes; but it won't scrap its old prejudices and its old moralities and its old religions and its old political constitutions' (*Major Barbara*, p. 328). Shaw is here very close to Bond who, in the Preface to *Saved*, argues: 'that means teaching, oddly enough, moral scepticism and analysis and not faith'. Such an attitude has no time for pessimism or outmoded romantic idealism, and the type of drama Shaw consequently evolved to express this clash of ideas similarly scorns neat theatrical conventions. The last act of *Major Barbara* works out the issues in envisaging a superman who will be a man of true vision: neither a romantic day-dreamer nor a ruthless pragmatist; as Undershaft puts it (in a significant addition in Shaw's revision of the play): 'Plato says, my friend, that society cannot be saved until either the Professors of Greek take to making gunpowder or else the makers of gunpowder become Professors of Greek' (p. 334). Andrew, the

armaments dealer, the practical man of action passes on his inheritance to Barbara, now freed from her blind idealism, and Cousins,
the Greek scholar and man of the world. We are made to feel that it
will descend to them and their children – as Bolingbroke's did to
Henry V – 'with better quiet, better opinion, better confirmation'.
Another Shakespearian reference is even more appropriate here.
The final twist of *Major Barbara* is that only a bastard (or found-
ling) can continue the Undershaft tradition and there is not a little
irony in the fact that Shaw – whose attitude to Shakespeare
throughout his career was profoundly ambivalent – should con-
clude this, his subtlest tragicomedy, with a philosophical paradox
identical to that expounded by Polixenes in Shakespeare's penultimate romance, *The Winter's Tale*:

> We marry
> A gentler scion to the wildest stock
> And make conceive a bark of baser kind
> By bud of nobler race. This is an art
> Which does mend nature – change it rather;
> But the art itself is nature.

(IV. iv. 92–7)

7
Twentieth-century pioneers

Everything is fable and everything is true, since it is inevitable that
we accept as true the empty appearances emanating from our
illusions and passions; to have illusions can be beautiful, but the
deception of too much fantasizing always results in tears. This
deception will appear to be comic or tragic depending on the degree
of our involvement with the vicissitudes of those who suffer the
deception, on the interest or sympathy which that passion and
illusion arouse in us, and on the effects that the deception produces.
(Luigi Pirandello, *On Humor*)

Chekhov and Shaw can be seen as the last romantics of European
drama. The contrasted emotions harmonized into a lyrical elegy
along with the recurrent themes of lost love, nostalgia and longing
for a better life make Chekhov's plays in mood and subject-matter
a requiem for a dying era. His drama is concerned with a world
which was doomed to end with the Russian Revolution of 1917,
and much of the emotional strength of his plays comes from the
pull between his sensitivity to the past and his hope for the future.
When Shaw looks to the past it is to find further material to support his attitude to the present and view of the future. There runs
through his work an evolutionary thesis which, as it is developed
from *Man and Superman* through *Major Barbara* to *Back to
Methuselah* gives them the coherence of a moral and philosophical
centre. It was his discovery of socialism in the 1890s which gave
Shaw the inspiration to turn from journalism and prose fiction to
the stage. It is his political awareness coupled with his faith in the
potential of humanity to develop into higher stages of evolution
which give force and credibility to his romantic optimism.

The political theory of Marx and the scientific discoveries of

Darwin taught Shaw to hope. Even the experience of the First World War, though it shook his faith temporarily, did not change his fundamental attitudes. But Darwin and Marx were to have much the same effect in the twentieth century as Galileo and Machiavelli in the Renaissance: they were seen to represent a dangerous challenge to orthodox religion and political faith. That man should be descended from the apes was even more damaging than that he should be displaced from the centre of the universe. The effect of Marx's political teachings was felt in Russia in 1917; the repercussions have developed continuously since. The committed political theatre consequent upon Brecht's conversion to Marxism in the late 1920s is very different from Shaw's drama of visionary socialism. Brecht was writing in the early 1930s to combat the rise of Nazism, but he was powerless to halt the success of Hitler and its consequences. The systematic genocide perpetrated by the Third Reich was equalled in horror only by the dropping of the atomic bomb at the end of the Second World War.

In discussing his protagonist in the Preface to *Galileo*, Brecht sees the atomic bomb as 'the classical end-product of his contribution to science and his failure to society'. Twentieth-century discoveries in physics have worked alongside nineteenth-century theories of natural science and political economy to change man's view of himself and the world. Einstein, whose research made possible the atomic bomb, has had a further influence on thought and philosophy. His theory of relativity has served to undermine man's spiritual and psychological confidence. Pirandello first explored the ludicrousness and torment brought about by the awareness of our personality as a mass of contradictions, our very existence qualified by the viewpoints and opinions of others. Einstein is said to have approached Pirandello after a performance of one of his plays and said: 'We are kindred souls.' Pirandello and Brecht respectively gave dramatic definition to the challenging new philosophical and political approaches of the inter-war period. They are joined by Artaud who, in his determination to return to myth in an exploration of the deepest roots of sexuality and violence, brought to the theatre the full force of Freud's disturbing psychological discoveries. The nightmare world of Artaud, the harsh truths of Brecht's social and political parables, and the bewildering shifts of perspective in Pirandello's dramas are different theatrical reflections of the doubts and confusions which characterized the first half of the century. It is a century which, as the corollary to its loss of faith, has witnessed the death of tragedy. Tragedy can only exist in a world with clearly defined ideals and absolutes. For Pirandello, Brecht and Artaud, tragedy was an even more inappropriate dramatic form than it had been for Chekhov and Shaw. These three dramatists are the major theatrical pioneers of the early twentieth century and in each case their innovations have had a pronounced influence on the development of tragicomedy.

Pirandello may at first seem the most significant creator of a mixed genre. But, of the three, his drama is closest to tragedy, while, as we shall see, there is a richer vein of comedy in Brecht and Artaud which is all too often underestimated. Pirandello's plays are rarely funny. But the theory of humour he both defined and developed in his drama is a vital contribution to our understanding of tragicomedy. Pirandello's lengthy study *On Humor* (1908) makes an interesting contrast with Bergson's *Laughter* (1900). Only the unavailability of the former in English translation until recently can account for its neglect, since it is as original and relevant to modern theatre as Bergson is conventional and outmoded. Pirandello's study anticipates the drama of the twentieth century; Bergson's looks back to the seventeenth. The depth and scope of *On Humor* may be seen in the range of Pirandello's references: from Chaucer and Boccaccio through Manzoni and Cervantes to Sterne and Swift. Bergson's are drawn exclusively from Molière and Labiche, with the important exception of Cervantes. But just as Bergson trivializes Molière's more complex dramas, *Tartuffe* and *Le Misanthrope*, while ignoring *Dom Juan*, he similarly relates *Don Quixote* to his own narrow definition. He maintains that 'the comic spirit has a logic of its own' and that 'laughter has no greater foe than emotion'. For him Don Quixote exemplifies 'systematic absentmindedness' which he sees as 'the most comical thing imaginable: it is the comic itself, drawn as nearly as possible from its very source' (*Laughter*, p. 146). Quixote bears out the truth of his theory that:

> Laughter is, above all, a corrective. Being intended to humiliate, it must make a powerful impression on the person against whom it is directed. By laughter society avenges itself for liberties taken with it. It would fail in its object if it bore the stamp of sympathy or kindness.
>
> (*Laughter*, p. 197)

Nothing could be further from Pirandello's point of view. For him, Quixote represents the existential crisis of Cervantes in which a writer acknowledges the conflict in his own life between idealism and the naked self which recognizes a world devoid of illusions. Pirandello, in his analysis of the Knight of the Woeful Countenance, is already anticipating his own creation, Henry IV. Tragedy and comedy are inseparable in Cervantes's recognition of himself in prison: 'He sees who he is and laughs at himself. All his sufferings burst into laughter' (*On Humor*, p. 88). Pirandello continues to deepen his analysis:

> How else could one explain the deep bitterness which, like a shadow, follows each step, each ridiculous act, each wild adventure that the poor Manchegan knight undertakes? It is the sense of grief that inspires the very image in the author when, substantiated as it is with his suffering, it wills itself as funny. And it wills itself so because reflection, the product of the most bitter experience has suggested to the author the *feeling of the opposite*, through which he recognizes his error and he wants to punish himself with the mockery that others will make of him.
>
> (p. 88)

The psychological and social implications of Pirandello's theory of humour are far more complex than Bergson's reflections on laughter. In seeing the difference between reality and the illusions which we cherish until they assume a reality of their own, the humourist does not merely laugh (like the comic writer) or feel superior (like the satirist): 'he will rather, in his laughter, feel compassion' (p. 89).

Pirandello goes on to provide a vivid example of the alternation and interdependence of a comic and tragic perspective in our perception of character and situation. His observations apply to the stage as well as to life.

> I see an old lady whose hair is dyed and completely smeared with some kind of horrible ointment; she is all made-up in a clumsy and awkward fashion and is all dolled-up like a young girl. I begin to laugh. I *perceive* that she is *the opposite* of what a respectable old lady should be. Now I could stop here at this initial and superficial comic reaction: the comic consists precisely of this *perception of the opposite*. But if at this point, reflection interferes in me to suggest that perhaps this old lady finds no pleasure in dressing up like an exotic parrot and perhaps that she is distressed by it and does it only because she pitifully deceives herself into believing that, by making herself up like that and by concealing her wrinkles and grey hair, she may be able to hold the love of her much younger husband – if reflection comes to suggest all this, then I can no longer laugh at her as I did at first, exactly because the inner working of reflection has made me go beyond, or rather enter deeper into, the initial stage of awareness: from the initial *perception of the opposite*, reflection has made me shift to a *feeling of the opposite*. And herein lies the precise difference between the comic and humour.
>
> (p. 113)

Pirandello provides a simpler example of how this process works when he goes on to discuss a poem by Giuseppe Giusti in which the writer, on seeing a group of soldiers from the occupying army in the Church of St Ambrogio in Milan, finds his feelings of hatred turn to sympathy (with men who are far from home and hated as foreigners) when he hears the strains of their solemn German hymn. This is an almost exact reversal of Brecht's *Verfremdungseffekt* (or alienation effect) in that Brecht seeks rather to staunch pity in an understanding of wider social and political issues. But Pirandello's concern to avoid a simplistic emotional response and emphasis on the relativity of feeling following a deepening awareness of a situation have an affinity with Brecht's technique.

Unlike his compatriot, Guarini, Pirandello's theory came before his practice but in both cases the two aspects are complementary. Moreover, there is in Pirandello's drama a control of emotion, a balance of feeling and thought, which, finding its verbal expression in the complex patterned rhythms of his rhetoric, is an extension of the neo-classicism of the Italian Renaissance. Pirandello's plays have the inevitability and precision of a calculated game of chess, but below the surface, threatening at all times to erupt, is a passionate undercurrent of feeling. Hence simultaneously we are drawn emotionally into the plays and kept at an intellectual distance. The effect of this constant shift of perspective means that we are made to sympathize with the situation in which the characters find themselves and yet we are made aware of the inherent absurdity of their predicament. It is a technique productive not so much of laughter as of comic dislocation. Like Shakespeare before him and Brecht after him, Pirandello was obsessed with the unreality of theatre as a mirror for the shifting realities of life. This is productive of the further ironies in his plays: the contrast between the stage world and the sordid events narrated and dramatized in *Six Characters in Search of an Author* (1921); the challenges based on misunderstanding alternating with the scenes in the foyer of the theatre in *Each in His Own Way* (1924); and the episodes in the story of passion re-created simultaneously in various parts of the theatre which serve to illustrate the theories of the bizarre director, Doctor Hinkfuss, in *Tonight We Improvise* (1930). *Henry IV* (1922) is the best known of Pirandello's plays outside Italy; it dramatizes the existential predicament of a man torn between reality and illusion, madness and sanity, preferring in the end the privacy of his own self-constructed world to the cruelty of the real world outside. He is simultaneously a tragic hero and a clown, both Hamlet and Petrouchka – as Felicity Firth, in the Introduction to *Three Plays* by Pirandello (Manchester, 1969, p. xxviii) has pointed out – his imperious conduct strangely at odds with his dyed hair and rouged cheeks. If Henry is the most strikingly modern of Pirandello's creations, it is the Father in *Six Characters in Search of an Author* who most precisely encapsulates his philosophy of human psychology:

> My drama lies entirely in this one thing . . . in my being conscious that each one of us believes himself to be a single person. But it's not true . . . each one of us is many persons. . . . Many persons . . . according to the possibilities of being that there are within us. . . . With some people we are one person. . . . With others we are somebody quite different. . . . And all the time we are under the illusion of always being one and the same person for everybody. . . . We believe that we are always this one person in whatever it is we may be doing. But it's not true! It's not true!
> (*Six Characters in Search of an Author*, p. 25)

Though his knowledge of the contradictions of personality and the relativity of action is tragic, the father's conduct is seen to be alternately pathetic and risible as the actors in turn try to re-create the traumatic sequence of events from which he cannot escape. The result is tragicomedy.

There is an interesting parallel here between Pirandello's method and Brecht's employment of the *Verfremdungseffekt*. A telling example of the latter is the sketch in *Fear and Misery in the Third Reich* (1938) in which a judge, faced with a difficult case, is variously seen speaking to a sequence of characters: a police officer, an ambitious counsel, a fellow judge, his housekeeper, his wife. Brecht wants us to see the issues from a carefully contrasted variety of angles; as in Pirandello's plays, the protagonist is seen to bare different, contradictory aspects of his personality in turn. Whereas Pirandello's concerns are existential, Brecht's are political.

He is not presenting a psychological development in his characters; each new perspective makes us revalue the situation. Though serving a serious, even didactic, purpose, this technique is essentially comic, as Brecht explained in discussing the first production:

> You saw the fear of the oppressed and the fear of the oppressors. It was like a great collection of gestures, observed with artistry . . . but what was so unusual was that the players never performed these ghastly episodes in such a way that the spectators were tempted to call out 'Stop!' The spectators didn't seem in any way to share the horror of those on stage, and as a result there was repeatedly laughter among the audience without doing any damage to the profoundly serious character of the performance. For this laughter seemed to apply to the stupidity that found itself having to make use of force, and to the helplessness that took the shape of brutality.
>
> *(Messingkauf Dialogues,* p. 72)

Many of the sketches in this work are funny, notably *The Spy* (number 10) in which a respectable couple bicker – in a manner which resembles characters in the plays of Brecht's English contemporaries Coward and Maugham – and then worry that their son, who has merely gone out to buy some chocolates, might be betraying their idle criticisms of the establishment to the SS. Brecht points an accusing finger at the complicity of the *petit bourgeoisie* who are just as much agents of Nazism as the Gestapo.

Brecht's criticism is the more effective because of his comic method. He himself stressed the importance of *Leichtigkeit* (lightness of touch) and *Spass* (fun) which the modern political dramatist ignores at his peril. 'A theatre that can't be laughed in', he claimed, 'is a theatre to be laughed at' *(Messingkauf Dialogues,* p. 95). Though comedy is handled with greater subtlety in the dramas written after his conversion to Marxism, it is also present in the earlier works. A savage humour pervades his first play *Baal* (1918) and is at its most intense in the scene with the woodcutters who are debating what to do about their fellow workman, Teddy.

Baal berates them for their lack of respect in drinking the dead man's own gin at his funeral, but it transpires that it was Baal who had previously stolen it, an irony made the more telling through the presence of the corpse and Baal's own clumsy manhandling of it. The horrific scenes of *Man Is Man* (1926) are also richly comic, notably the mutilation of Jip and the castration of Bloody Five and – as with the drama of Bond – they carry a deeper moral and political meaning. The grotesque humour of the piece presents in fact a nightmarish world, like that of *Baal*, which breaks down psychological certainties and transforms a peace-loving innocent into an inhuman fighting machine. *The Resistible Rise of Arturo Ui* (1941) reveals Brecht at his most skilful as a satirist. His relish in the comic-strip presentation of the rise of Ui, the gangster, is matched by a clever handling of parody – features which have influenced modern playwrights such as David Edgar in *Dick Deterred* (an attack on Nixon). The contrast between the comic machinations of Ui and the real-life manoeuvres of Hitler are emphasized by the fact that, at least in the earlier part of the play, the actual political events are described on slides while a farcical travesty of them is enacted in front of us. When the two levels meet, however, they do so with chilling effect, as in the scene with the ham actor which starts off as the broadest parody of outmoded classical acting but ends with the stunning physical stage image of his transformation into the goose-stepping, ranting figure of the Führer.

Brecht claimed that 'modern theatre is Epic Theatre' and went on to explain (in the notes to *Mahagonny*) the 'shift of accent' which such an approach demanded. Whereas Dramatic Theatre (notably tragedy) relies on plot, placing the audience in the passive role of spectator, Epic Theatre relies on narrative, involving the audience as observer and arousing its power of action. While drama implies that the audience have their eyes on the finish as one scene develops into another in a process of growth, epic requires the audience to have their eyes on the course, each scene working for itself in a process of montage. Like Pirandello and

Artaud, Brecht had no time for the psychological clichés of conventional theatre. He argued:

> You can't give a realistic picture of the character you are putting
> forward for identification (the hero) without making it imposs-
> ible for the audience to identify itself with him. A realistic pic-
> ture would mean that he had to change with events which would
> make him too unreliable for such empathy; he would also have a
> very limited viewpoint, which would mean that the spectator
> who shared it would not see far enough.
>
> (*Messingkauf Dialogues*, p. 26)

Brecht's 'realistic picture' is established through techniques which
Bergson felt to be the prerogative of the writer of comedy. Bergson
insists on the value of comedy as a social corrective and argues:
'Method and object are here of the same nature as in the inductive
sciences, in that observation is always external and the result
always general' (*Laughter*, p. 169). Brecht's aim, however, is more
precise. His rejection of naturalism and tragedy in favour of Epic
Theatre resulted in a mixed genre which had immense critical
potential and which has developed in the contemporary theatre
into a vital and important variation of tragicomedy.

Like Brecht, Artaud intended his drama to shock. His emphasis,
however, is emotional. The influence of his concept of a Theatre
of Cruelty on modern directors and playwrights has been out of all
proportion to his own severely limited achievement. He was clear
what this theatre should do, stating: 'Let us not be mistaken,
cruelty for me has nothing to do with blood or duty . . . it means
doing everything the director can to the sensibilities of actor and
spectator' (*Le Petit Parisien*, 14 April 1935). In his disastrous
career he attempted to realize this new concept of drama, one free
of the limitations imposed by psychological naturalism or printed
script. Contemptuous of 'those creepy men, otherwise known as
playwrights', he asked: 'How can it be that in the theatre . . . in the
West, everything specifically theatrical, that is to say everything that
cannot be expressed in words . . . has been left in the background?'

(*The Theatre and Its Double*, London, 1970, p. 26). And he demanded 'Whoever said theatre was made to define a character, to
resolve conflicts of human emotional order, of a present day
psychological nature such as those which monopolise current
theatre?' (p. 30). What Artaud advocated was a theatre of mixed
means, not merely a fusion of contrasted dramatic forms but an
amalgam of every stage technique available. His experiments are
therefore important not only in the context of theatrical history
but also in the development of modern tragicomedy.

Artaud's first steps towards achieving his aim were his productions for the Alfred Jarry Theatre in June 1927. He took the
name of the anarchic author of the Ubu plays, a precursor of the
Dadaist and Surrealist movements, as his inspiration for mounting
a series of performances which were early examples of the 'hap-
pening', a phenomenon which swept America in the 1960s. The
first programme consisted of Artaud's *Acid Stomach or the Mad
Mother*, 'a comic exposition of the clash between theatre and the
cinema', Roger Vitrac's *The Secrets of Love*, 'an ironic play, physically staging the misgivings, dual isolation, eroticism and criminal
thoughts lurking in the minds of lovers', and *Gigoyne* by Max
Robur (the pseudonym of Robert Aron), 'written and produced
with the deliberate aim of needling people' (*Collected Works*, II,
pp. 33–4). Three other programmes followed, ranging from satiric
mockery in Claudel's *Partage de Midi* to the offensively farcical in
Vitrac's *Victor*, which concerns a heroine unable to control her
wind in polite company. 'Nothing was spared', comments Victor
Corti, 'living room drama was mercilessly satirized, verse drama
ridiculed, the stage became a provocation and Naturalism the
visual subconscious' (*Collected Works*, II, p. 7). This early
theatrical enterprise proved to be totally unsuccessful, however,
largely because Artaud had not discovered – as directors since have
more effectively succeeded in doing – a directing style which could
do justice to the work. Rejecting any approach that was either
coherent or conventional, he called for 'quick fire dialogue, stock
characters, swift movement, stereotyped attitudes, proverbial

expressions, comic songs, grand opera, etc.' (II, p. 38). He was clearer about his aim, however. He wanted not only 'total theatre' but 'total laughter', a far cry from Brecht's twin concepts of *Spass* and *Leichtigkeit*, as can be seen from his description: 'laughter extending from paralyzed slavvering to convulsed, side-holding sobbing' (II, p. 38).

Artaud's impatience with the craft of play writing, resulting from his own psychological problem of communication, led him to compose scenarios for both the screen and stage. In these he was more at liberty than in a more formally constructed play to crowd together his disparate and elliptical images, while the need to provide a sequence of visual effects was more pressing than the obligation to write dialogue. *The Spurt of Blood*, an attack on all accepted values, is both a revelation of Artaud's inner life and an important link between the Surrealist movement and the Theatre of the Absurd. Alternating between a peaceful scene involving two lovers and the eruption on to the stage of a representative group of figures – Priest, Cobbler, Beadle, Judge, Whore and Barrow-Woman – in grotesque combination, it climaxes in a terrifying thunderstorm in which a huge hand seizes the whore's hair which catches fire as she cries out, 'God, let go of me!' and bites the hand, thus causing 'a great spurt of blood to slash across the stage'. More important for the purpose of this study is *The Philosopher's Stone*. This piece, having its roots in stage conventions as distinct from poetic or pictorial art, is more susceptible to theatrical representation. It is a demented *commedia dell' arte* sketch expressed in the manner of Grand Guignol. As the peculiarly Gallic form of the Grand Guignol developed in France at the turn of the century, its leading themes, according to Frantisek Deak, became: 'death, crime and insanity . . . tempered with sex, adultery, vengeance, hypnotism, surgical operations and torture' ('Théâtre du Grand Guignol', *The Drama Review*, XLVI, 39). Each of these elements is present in *The Philosopher's Stone*, which shows how Harlequin, having wormed his way into the laboratory of the sinister Doctor Pale, is dismembered only to resurrect himself miraculously and seduce Isabella while the doctor sleeps. What is more significant is that Artaud here achieves theatrical precision in his employment of two sharply contrasted dramatic genres and in so doing provides us with an example of how two such opposed theatrical conventions as farce and melodrama can be combined to powerful and disturbing effect.

It is revealing to compare the three dramatists discussed above with Ionesco and Beckett, the two important exponents of the Theatre of the Absurd which came into vogue after the Second World War. Pirandello's tragicomic figures are precursors of the anti-heroes of the Absurdists and there are parallels between the surreal effects in the work of Artaud and Ionesco. In the 1950s, however, the philosophical disillusionment of the post-war playwrights was given more precise definition in a powerful new variety of the mixed genre. The *raison d'être* of this theatre is explained by Leonard Cabell Pronko at the end of his extensive study:

> In a universe without absolutes tragedy is impossible. In such a universe pure comedy is no longer possible either, for man seems to belong nowhere, is the constituent of no hierarchy, either divine or social. Man examines himself as a peculiar suffering animal in the zoological garden of the world, and the result is often amusing. But when he turns to the infinities that surround him, the result is disquieting. Precisely because the dramatists of the avant-garde usually see man not only in a horizontal context, but in the vertical one as well, they blend the amusing with the disquieting. Those who are the most hopelessly pessimistic and the most clearly 'meta-physical' are often the most laughable, perhaps because their pessimism leaves them no recourse but laughter. Pessimism, like a double negative, can after all negate itself into something resembling an affirmative: if everything is so futile and meaningless, and yet life is all we have, we may as well make the best of it we can, laughing not only at the ridiculous spirit of seriousness in others, but at our own disillusionment.
>
> (*Avant-Garde: The Experimental Theatre in France*,
> p. 205)

Eugène Ionesco was the first dramatist to emerge from this school and he seems superficially to have a good deal in common with Artaud. Certainly he too is much concerned in his plays with 'the cruelty objects can practise on us': in several of his dramas objects take on a life of their own, as in *The Chairs* (1952) in which an Old Man and an Old Woman are busily engaged in lining up a row of chairs which are subsequently occupied by invisible auditors for a lecture. Unlike Godot, the Orator finally arrives but when he speaks, 'from his throat come moans and groans and the sort of guttural sounds made by deaf mutes' (p. 22). Many of Ionesco's early plays have affinities with the scenarios Artaud devised for his Theatre of Cruelty: they have a surreal logic, a deliberate refusal to present events in any straightforward, naturalistic way. His first play, the short piece *The Bald Prima Donna* (1950), effectively launched Absurd Theatre. In it events occur as haphazardly and meaninglessly as in Artaud's *The Spurt of Blood*: an ordinary English couple, Mr and Mrs Martin, who do not recognize one another though they have lived together for many years are joined by a fireman who answers the door bell the fourth time it is rung, thereby proving Mrs Smith's point: 'When you hear a ring at the door, it means there's never anyone there' (*The Bald Prima Donna*, p. 101). The inconsequentiality of the piece – notably the series of illogical tales the characters in turn narrate – develops towards the furious dénouement in which the characters 'all together, at the top of their bent, scream into each other's ears, getting faster and faster, then fading away as the LIGHTS dim to BLACK OUT' (p. 119).

In his essay 'Experience of the theatre' published in *Notes and Counter Notes*, Ionesco explains his aesthetic, a vital contribution to the tragicomic genre:

It seems to me that the comic is tragic, and that the tragedy of man is pure derision. The contemporary critical mind takes nothing too seriously or too lightly. In *Victims of Duty* I tried to sink comedy in tragedy: in *The Chairs* tragedy in comedy, or if you like to confront comedy and tragedy in order to link them in a new dramatic synthesis. But it is not a true synthesis for these two elements do not coalesce, they coexist: one constantly repels the other, they show each other up, criticize and deny one another and thanks to their opposition thus succeed dynamically in maintaining a balance and creating tension.

(London, 1964, p. 27)

In a series of plays written during the 1950s and culminating in the production of *Rhinoceros* in 1960, Ionesco explored this vision of a mad world in which events are simultaneously alarming and ludicrous. In *The Lesson* (1951) an apparently innocent young girl and an apparently harmless old professor enact a ritual which is by turns comic, pathetic, grotesque and horrifying, culminating in murder, but which appears more profoundly disturbing when the Maid shows in another pupil as the curtain falls. In *Amédée or How to Get Rid of It* (1954) an off-stage corpse gradually grows and develops, obtruding its presence more and more into the 'unpretentious dining room, drawing room and office combined' which forms the setting for the first two acts.

In *Rhinoceros* Ionesco reveals the headlong lunacy of civilization through the eyes of his hero, Bérenger, who is compelled to see everyone around him gradually transformed into rhinoceroses. He refuses to join the stampede to destruction, finally determined after looking at himself in the mirror and bemoaning his smooth brow, limp hands and slack skin to 'take on the whole lot of them'. His stand represents that of modern man: though he is denied the dignity of a tragic stature he is at the same time desperate in his awareness of the impossible position forced on him. He is an archetypal figure of tragicomedy and it is significant that he should recur in the last of Ionesco's major dramas *Exit the King*, written two years later in 1962. Now Bérenger is king, though still a figure representative of humanity. Here he is forced to come to terms with the ultimate reality, death. Ionesco's first play, *The Bald Prima Donna*, had at its roots a verbal comedy; it represented for the author 'the death of language'. *Exit the King* is also a very verbal piece. It has the economy of means and the inevitability of a Racinian tragedy though many of its effects are closer to the comedy of Molière. The 'derisory royal music' which is an imitation of that composed for the ceremony of the king's rising prepares us for the ironic tone of this tragicomedy about a dying monarch. The play, however, represents a neat reversal of the features so characteristic of Ionesco's previous drama in that the basic principle here is one of renunciation, of rejection of all diversions and consequently of all stage effects. As the play ends, Bérenger, guided by the faithful Marguerite, has relinquished all physical things: those objects which represented such terrors to Artaud and to Amédée or Bérenger himself in his previous incarnation now cannot touch him; he finally abandons even his own limbs one by one and, himself now an abstraction, slowly fades from our sight. This final *coup de théâtre* – and with it the gradual disappearance of all the scenic decoration – fittingly constitutes our last glimpse of Ionesco's existential hero. Throughout the play his orders have been disregarded by the elements and the members of his court; this makes him appear alternately pathetic and risible. Like Beckett's Hamm he becomes immobile, his throne converted to a wheelchair; like Pozzo he goes blind; finally he faces the inevitability, at once tragic and ridiculous, of his own dissolution.

The savage physical and emotional emphasis of Artaud's theatre finds an echo in the drama of Ionesco but is conspicuously lacking in the plays of Beckett. Indeed Beckett has pared down his effects over the years, thus gradually getting further and further away from the sort of staging envisaged by Artaud. By contrast Beckett's theatre is one of marked restraint. This is true even of his first and by far his most exuberant play, *Waiting for Godot* (1955), which he termed 'a tragicomedy in two acts'. 'Nothing happens, nobody comes, nobody goes, it's awful': Beckett disarms criticism from the start. But in fact – certainly compared with the plays which were to follow – a great deal happens, even if it is confined to the (repeated) exits and entrances of a small group of characters.

Indeed in Guarinian or Aristotelian terms nothing happens: the play's originality lies precisely in giving theatrical definition to existential awareness of the Death of Time and the futility of all action. Nor are the characters represented with any psychological definition since their natures are subject to the relative awareness of others. Having thus discarded all the conventional prerequisites of drama, Beckett proceeds to entertain us with verbal and (in this play) physical variations on his theme performed by two contrasted comic double acts. As Kenneth Tynan pointed out (of the one Beckett play he truly admired): 'the play sees the human condition in terms of baggy pants and red noses . . . for the most part [Beckett's tramps] converse in the double talk of vaudeville' (*A View of the English Stage*, London, 1975, p. 106).

In his novel *Watt* (1953) Beckett analyses several kinds of laughter, all of which have a serious or tragic undertow. He distinguishes between three basic types: 'the bitter laugh that laughs at that which is not good', the intellectually based 'hollow laugh' which 'laughs at that which is not true', and the laugh of laughs, the 'risus purus' which has as its source 'that which is unhappy' (p. 47). Such careful definition extends the implications of Guarini's *Compendio* via the theorizing of Bergson and Pirandello into a modern existential concept. All three types of laughter are to be found in *Godot*. An example of the 'bitter laugh' is jesting about something as grimly serious and potentially tragic as suicide, as death seems the only release from the eternal meaningless waiting. At the beginning of Act II occurs an example of the 'hollow laugh' where, in Vladimir's insistence that Estragon say he is happy, we are presented with a verbal repartee grown stale by repetition. It has the force of a catechism, though the last thing it achieves is faith. It is none the less funny on stage precisely because there is such a powerful build-up of the carefully balanced phrases which collapse in the bathos of the conclusion. The 'risus purus' is reserved for the climactic moment of the play where Beckett can the more forcefully combine comedy and tragedy. In so far as the play has any linear development, it is from comedy to tragedy, not vice versa. Bit by bit the comic potential of the jokes is exhausted and by the time Act II has run its course the inevitability of waiting and failure is established. Act II repeats much of the material of Act I but things are now markedly worse: Lucky is dumb, Pozzo blind and the tedious repetitiousness of life enforces the concept of Pozzo's 'accursed time'. At the end of the play Vladimir makes one more attempt to animate the now stale joke with a hat, then a last variation on the sad gag of his fallen trousers gives way to the ultimate 'risus purus', the confounding of all action.

Beckett's dramatic development since *Godot* has been an inexorable one. If this first play seemed to discard the basic raw materials of theatre he has since deliberately limited his effects to an even greater extent by restricting the mobility of his characters and by moving gradually away from any form of dialogue to soliloquy. When asked whether he felt he had been consciously influenced by Beckett, Tom Stoppard informed me that he, along with fellow dramatists like Pinter, had learnt something from Beckett in that before him it was accepted that theatre needed a basic ingredient – x – as a minimum to provide theatrical interest. It was Beckett who taught new writers that theatre could work with what we might term x minus 5. Stoppard added, more significantly, that Beckett had gone on to prove that theatre could manage with x minus 50 though he (Stoppard) had lost him somewhere around x minus 25. The complex patterns of sound and movement generated in *Godot* have the force of choreography; this is severely restricted in his next play, *Endgame* (1957), where Hamm is obliged to remain seated, Clov to keep on the move, while Nagg and Nell live in bins, like so much refuse, a stage to which the other two will come. The economy of dramatic means is taken further in *Happy Days* (1961) which shows us the central character, Winnie, at first buried up to her waist in sand, then – in the second act – buried up to her neck. Relentlessly she sifts through the clutter of objects in her 'capacious black bag' until, in the second part of the play, she is left with only her memories. Willie, who emerges briefly from his hole, provides even less contact than that offered to Hamm by his servant Clov.

As if to isolate his characters still further and deny them the comfort of verbal exchanges, however vacuous, in his next drama *Play* (1963) we are shown the three unnamed figures embedded in urns, each uttering brief snatches of talk, unaware of each other's presence. The *ne plus ultra* must surely be *Not I* (1973), a technical *tour de force* for writer and actress, in which the audience sees only a mouth desperately pouring out its tormented, repetitive confession while a dimly glimpsed figure looks on. Beckett's development fascinatingly parallels Chekhov's in his remorseless elimination of action, here carried to a greater extreme. Both writers are fusing the comic and the tragic in their presentation of the essential ambiguity of the human predicament through increasingly sophisticated experiments in dramatic form.

As Beckett's theatrical techniques have grown more extreme, so his development from *Godot* to *Not I* reveals a refinement of his lyrical skills. We cannot fully appreciate his later works unless we look at them from a poetic, even a musical, viewpoint. The early play for radio *All That Fall* (1957) reveals Beckett's first attempt to orchestrate a series of brief conversations (here spoken by fully rounded characters) with 'rural sounds: sheep, bird, cow, cock, severally then together', physical noises (footsteps, bicycle bell, car and train) and brief snatches of music (specifically here Schubert's *Death and the Maiden*). The narrative – of an old, infirm, overweight woman going to meet her blind husband – has elements of the ridiculous and the sad which are interwoven throughout with a musical precision and richness. Since there is a warmth in the characterization here, the comedy is often gentler than in the stage works; there are in fact strong echoes of Dylan Thomas and his 'play for voices', *Under Milk Wood*. Gradually, over the years, Beckett's stage plays have returned more and more to the musicality of *All That Fall*. The more characters have become circumscribed in their actions, the more Beckett has been able to extend the sound qualities of language: the rhythms, the constant repetitions in the manner of musical leitmotifs and variations, the precise organization of groups of words and the contrasts between separate vocal sections. The culmination of this technique is *Not I* which matches the inexorable reduction of stage effects with a concomitant precision of language so as to extend the dramatic form of tragicomedy into something more closely resembling music theatre.

8
Old ways, new directions

> *Waters.* It's not the jokes. It's not the jokes. It's what lies behind
> 'em. It's the attitude. A real comedian – that's a daring man. He
> *dares* to see what his listeners shy away from, fear to express. And
> what he sees is a sort of truth, about people, about their situation,
> about what hurts or terrifies them, about what's hard, above all,
> about what they *want*. A joke releases the tension, says the unsay-
> able, any joke pretty well. But a true joke, a comedian's joke, has
> to do more than release tension, it has to *liberate* the will and the
> desire, it has to *change the situation*.
>
> (Trevor Griffiths, *Comedians*)

In this study we have examined the emergence of a critical theory
of tragicomedy in the sixteenth century and its appropriateness as
a guide to evaluate the skills of neo-classical dramatists from
Shakespeare to Corneille. In contrast to this neo-classical approach
is the satiric, the ironic, which – notably in the plays of the revenge
convention from Marlowe onwards – seeks to undermine the
serious emotional and ethical issues through scenes of bathos,
parody and low comedy. When we reach the late nineteenth and
early twentieth centuries there is a parallel conflict of approaches
which expresses itself in a pull between the romantic and the
realistic. Melodrama, which developed out of the Romantic movement, can lend itself to escapist fantasy, or to socially and politically subversive theatre depending on whether the writer is
Boucicault or John Walker. This genre was refined in the plays of
Chekhov and Shaw, who fused realism and romance and in so
doing developed a vital and influential type of tragicomedy. The
theatrical pioneers of the inter-war period discovered fresh theatrical forms to give this clash of values new definition and meaning.

The student of post-war drama, therefore, is faced with a bewildering variety of theatrical idioms all of which fall into the category of a mixed dramatic genre. Some guidance as to the reasons for the predominance and diversity of tragicomedy in contemporary theatre can be gleaned from the studies of Cyrus Hoy and J. L. Styan. But they do not place the modern examples in a broader perspective of tragicomedy, an omission which is the more striking when we consult such surveys as that of Marvin T. Herrick which is restricted to the neo-classical period. The present study is the first to examine tragicomedy over a wider period and to compare the theatrical forms which represent its most significant expression. We must now look back over the range of plays we have considered and ask by what criteria we should evaluate the work of contemporary writers in this field, considering to what extent the formulations advanced to justify the genre when it first came to prominence are valid as critical tools for the student of twentieth-century theatre.

It may at first be thought that the purpose of Guarini's formulations in the *Compendio* is merely a justification of dramatic form. The somewhat stilted nature of *Il Pastor Fido*, a work which developed during a long period of gestation, seems to attest to this, being as much a justification of a theory as a vital theatrical piece in its own right. But Guarini was concerned with more than form. The 'structural aim' of the writer is subservient to the 'overall' one: the real justification of tragicomedy is cathartic: it 'purges with delight the melancholy of the audience'. This may seem a little like special pleading, too slavish an adherence to an Aristotelian line of argument, the end too glibly justifying the means. But we move well outside the literary implications of dramatic theory when we observe the influence of Guarini on Shakespeare and Corneille. The latter, in translating the clash of tragedy and comedy into a fusion of passion and intellect, presenting characters who control potentially destructive forces through reason and compassion, is reflecting the ethical and political views of his society. Shakespeare in the romances, and particularly in *The Tempest*, is doing more than modifying literary and theatrical material to evolve a new dramatic form of his own. He is attempting to present a picture of the world as he sees it, a picture developed from the tragic vision of the earlier plays.

Tragedy is concerned with waste and destruction. It views man as ultimately corruptible, doomed, whether by his own nature or by forces beyond his control. In Shakespeare's tragedies comedy does nothing to alleviate the pathos and the terror: it serves to heighten it. Comedy carried to its logical conclusion in farce is in some senses even more pessimistic. It sees the intransigent folly of man and is concerned with his inability to change. In the plays of Plautus, Molière and Feydeau, man is programmed. In Molière's complex emotional dramas – the great trio written in the mid-1660s – the endings are more despairing and bleak: Tartuffe's machinations are most implausibly halted; Juan is condemned to hell; and Alceste, the misanthrope, renounces the world. Tragicomedy sees the evil, the corrupt potential of humanity, the danger; but refuses to accept that it must triumph. Hence in Chekhov characters cling, however vainly, to a thin hope; they are tenacious to the end. Chekhov's conversion of the melodrama formula is matched by Shaw who employs it to provoke questions, to ask whether particular evils cannot be cured by attacking the problem at its root.

It is when we examine the basic aims of contemporary dramatists that we can take the essence of Guarini's approach and employ it to explore the nature of modern tragicomedy and its links with past theatrical forms. Edward Bond has a great deal in common with both Shaw and Chekhov. He has stated that he is an optimist by nature but a pessimist by experience. Hence – like Shaw and Chekhov – he can portray evil and destruction realistically in both a personal and a political context and yet see beyond it. He is closer to Shaw than Chekhov in his social and political ideology; he can see beyond the 'tinpot little tragedies' with which naturalistic theatre concerns itself to the greater political evil and its cure. His method is closer still to Brecht in his use of techniques from Epic Theatre, particularly in his recent plays. Where Shaw's emphasis is verbal, Bond's is physical: as in the stoning of the baby in *Saved* (1965), a play which provides us with a fine example of modern tragicomedy. This drama has a great deal in common with Shaw's *Mrs Warren's Profession*, another play banned by the censor on account of its unpalatable presentation of social evils. Like Shaw, Bond works by a method of dramatic paradox. The point is made in the quotation from Blake quoted in the programme: 'Sooner murder an infant in its cradle than nurse unacted desires'. The play does not support violence, rather it demands to know – as Shaw did – what are the greater social and political evils which make it inevitable, like prostitution. Bond's point – and his hope for the future – is made through a dramatic structure which echoes that outlined by Guarini. As he explains in the preface: 'By not playing the traditional role in the tragic Oedipus pattern of the play, Len turns it into what is formally a comedy' (*Saved*, pp. 5–6).

Bond is closer to Guarini in his basic dramatic aim. He does not so much seek to purge with delight the melancholy of the audience as to instil in the theatre goer a more profound sense of hope. Only by confronting issues as they really are, by facing people at their worst and learning from experience, is there a way forward. Hence the hero's dogged insistence on mending the chair in the final scene – a tableau of stark dramatic force interrupted only by Len's terse 'Fetch me 'ammer' – is a true affirmation of optimism. This is why Bond regards *Saved* as 'almost irresponsibly optimistic' and why in both dramatic form and ethical intention it represents a logical extension of the aims of neo-classical tragicomedy.

Bond also has much in common with Shakespeare. If we examine the romances carefully we observe a gradual tempering of the fairy-tale element with a realistic acceptance of man's potential. In *The Tempest* the narrative is grounded in the immediate historical fact of the accounts of travellers to the Bermudas, while Prospero's magic is severely circumscribed. On one level the ending of the play is bleak: Sebastian and Antonio will not repent, Caliban is unchangeable. In *Bingo* Bond suggests that Shakespeare took his own life as a result of his guilty sense of economic and political compromise; we need not go as far as this to realize that the positive values extolled in Shakepeare's final plays are all the more credible because they are balanced by reality and stem inevitably from his own experience and development. It is revealing that Shakespeare should have returned to the subject-matter of *King Lear* in his last creative phase and made it basic to all these dramas. It is indeed a crucial play in the development of tragicomedy. Itself a mixture of theatrical extremes, it expresses a tragic view of life with greater intensity and on a bigger scale than any other of his dramas. Yet it is itself an adaptation of a tragicomedy: the source play *The Chronicle History of King Lear*. Shakespeare chose to give expression to the intensity of his own despair through his treatment of the anonymous drama. Bond has expressed his own need to work through Shakespeare's tragedy in his own *Lear* (1971) before he could develop further. Shakespeare's drama has also been profoundly influential on Beckett who – in *Endgame* most notably – has echoed many of his theatrical devices in his own absurd vision of a tragicomic world.

In the savage farce of Marlowe, the dramas of the revenge convention and those tragedies intercut with flashes of comedy, there is a tradition of tragicomic writing in the late Elizabethan and early Jacobean period which is profoundly pessimistic. This is the subject of Chapter 3 and offers a contrast with the idyllic escapist genre of neo-classical pastoral and romance. The attitude to life of Marlowe, Webster, Middleton – and Shakespeare in his central, tragic phase – is savage and negative. The satires they created are an important variation of tragicomedy and have also influenced contemporary writers. Peter Barnes continues this tradition of satire, which was inherited from the Jacobeans and also has much in common with Artaud's Theatre of Cruelty in that it aims to 'launch repeated bayonet attacks on naturalism' (Introduction, *Collected Plays*, p. ix). Barnes explains his techniques and objectives in the preface to his one-act play *Leonardo's Last Supper* which mixes slapstick comedy and coarse farce with stark horror:

> Nothing a writer can imagine is as surrealistic as the reality. Everything has happened ... and so the aim is to create, by means of soliloquy, rhetoric, formalized ritual, slapstick, songs and dances, a comic theatre of contrasting moods and opposites where everything is simultaneously tragic and ridiculous.
>
> (p. 122)

Like Artaud, Barnes sees the world as mad and it is his intention to drive home to his audience a full awareness of this folly. No play does this more powerfully than *Laughter* (1978), a double bill in which the violence perpetrated by Ivan the.Terrible is matched by an account of Nazi atrocities in the concentration camps. It would be difficult to find themes further from the traditional realm of comedy; indeed in making these issues of overwhelming horror and world-wide tragedy funny Barnes is pushing the implications of tragicomedy to their limit. As against Brecht's technique of handling serious political themes with satirical lightness, he applies a battery of Artaud-style effects, grimly serious and hilariously comic by turns, to shock us into an awareness of the potentiality of human cruelty. Throughout both parts the phrase 'Root it out' is repeated again and again as a reminder of the impossibility of controlling either laughter or evil. The second play, *Auschwitz*, begins as a typical situation comedy set in an office on Christmas Eve and ridiculing the inanities of bureaucracy. When we learn that the workers are responsible for handling the orders of Cyclone B, the gas used in the extermination camps, the savagery of the humour gradually deepens. Neither the descriptions of the deranged Nazi, Gottlieb, nor the physical enactment of events before the eyes of the staff will make them accept the truth. Instead they turn to the audience and sing a song from *How to Succeed in Business without Really Trying*; this is followed by the ultimate in grim humour: a pair of Jewish comedians in prison-camp uniform performing a comic routine about death to the tune of 'On the sunny side of the street' as they are gassed. The full emotional potential of Artaud's theatre of mixed means is here given an added dimension of ethical and political relevance.

What is important here in our consideration of tragicomedy, however, is the author's attitude to humour. Barnes asks in the Prologue, 'In the face of Attila the Hun, Ivan the Terrible, a Passendale or Auschwitz, what good is laughter?' (*Laughter*, p. 343). His Author maintains that 'Laughter is the ally of tyrants. It softens our hatred. An excuse to change nothing, for nothing needs changing when it's all a joke.' This firm belief and his determination at all costs to 'Root it out' are mocked by a sequence of comic gags: a custard pie hits him in the face, his bow tie spins round and his trousers fall down. Laughter is more volatile. It will not submit to the rules laid down by Bergson or Meredith. It arises with disturbing force on the most unexpected occasions. Barnes's theatrical techniques serve to beg more aggressively the questions raised by Pirandello in *On Humor* and to remind us that in evaluating the methods and aims of modern dramatists his findings are a contemporary counterpart to those of Guarini. Pirandello is less prescriptive in his essay; it was written before his experience of creating plays. But the two together provide us with a key to the contemporary tragicomedies which are concerned with the ambiguity of personality and situation and focusing on this problem through new theatrical techniques.

There is a Pirandellian awareness of the unreality of feeling and its corollary is the complex relationship of the tragic to the comic in Bri, the central character of Peter Nichols's play: *A Day in the Death of Joe Egg*. Both this play and this dramatist are important and useful in a discussion of modern tragicomedy since they ask important questions about the purpose of this contemporary genre. Alternating between his chats to Joe, the human vegetable who is his child, and his conversations with the audience, Bri tells us:

I can't sustain a passion to the end of the sentence. I start to cry
– aaaoooow! Then I think: are you mad? What do you think you

are, God? And things go clang and wheels fall off and people get hurt – terrible. You must have felt like this – catching yourself in the mirror hamming away. Or somebody says, 'My wife's just been run over' and you want to burst out laughing. Well you may say, why not, if that's the way you feel. But other people don't like it. So I pretend. You saw me pretend with Sheila. I try to guess which emotions appeal to her and then sink my teeth in. I don't let go until they're bone dry. Like with Joe there – [*waves to her*]. All right are you? Good. I felt all doomy at first but – well – ten years! I just go through the motions now.

(pp. 25–6)

Though all Nichols's plays can be termed comedies, the subject-matter is never that traditionally associated with the form. His themes – which range from the problems of raising a mentally handicapped child to the Opium Wars between the British and the Chinese – may properly be thought to be the province of tragedy. In a previous age this would have been so, but the modern theatre which has risen to a stature befitting the gravity of the century's events only in such works as Peter Weiss's *The Investigation*, can no longer treat the merely personal as an issue worthy of tragedy. Weiss's play diminishes the attempts of writers – notably in America – to bring dignity and meaning to the fate of the individual. The only approach to problems of a human psychological nature is one which abandons the pretensions of tragedy and extends its pity into laughter.

Nichols and Barnes are both writers who challenge the boundaries of the comic. In so doing they inevitably break down conventional dramatic forms. Neither is a naturalistic dramatist. But Chekhov continues to influence British theatre, in the mature plays of John Osborne, the work of David Storey, and the dramas of Simon Gray, for instance. Naturalism, since it seeks to convey the multiplicity of human experience, must by its very nature be tragi-comic. Since the above writers are concerned essentially with the individual and with psychological relationships, their plays are – at least in terms of basic aims – compatible with Guarinian theory. But when we consider artists who employ theatrical stylizations which are both related to more popular, less literary traditions of theatre and influenced by the discoveries of the inter-war pioneers, we can no more usefully apply a literary theory to their work than to that of Marlowe or Webster. The student of modern drama needs instead to concern himself with different criteria. He must consider more closely the relationship between actor and audience and ask how the theatrical techniques of the writer are used to disturb. He needs to examine how the writer seeks to subvert psychological, ethical and political beliefs rather than to bolster them through empathy and catharsis.

Influential dramatic critics from Aristotle to Bergson share certain vital assumptions. Their theories are dependent on the unfolding of a complex plot, the development of character, and the clarity of moral issues. The manipulation of the audience's emotional responses in Guarini's theory of tragicomedy is equally bound up with these three features. Modern theatre, however, has gone a considerable way to destroying all of them. The Absurdists, notably Beckett, continued a tendency observable in the plays of Chekhov to pare the action down to the barest minimum. The major axis of Brecht's theory of Epic Theatre rests on a substitution of narrative for plot, a concentration on montage rather than growth, a focus on the course, not the finish. Now human nature is inevitably seen in a post-Freudian, post-Einsteinian world as variable and volatile. Nor can ethical and moral absolutes be taken for granted. In the twentieth century the villain has changed. For Beckett, he is 'accursed time'; for Artaud, 'society' which is 'iniquitous and ought to be destroyed'; for Brecht and Bond, more specifically the capitalist state.

The strength of modern drama resides chiefly in its discovery of fresh theatrical structures which serve a serious ethical and social purpose. On the one hand are writers like Beckett and Pirandello who seek to pinpoint and fix some meaning on the bewildering contradictions in life by offering through the theatrical medium some sense of definition and thus of permanence and sense. On the other hand are writers like Barnes and Bond who wish to make the play goer more aware of political issues. The theatre continues to act as a mirror and as a catalyst, and we can best understand the aim of the writer of modern tragicomedy in the light of this. We need to concentrate less on matters of dramatic form, therefore, and more on the theatrical medium employed. A real evaluation of the methods of contemporary playwrights will only come about when the student of the modern stage has learnt to shift his focus of attention from a consideration of tragedy and comedy as literary and dramatic genres to an evaluation of laughter and anger as intellectual and emotional responses to theatrical effects.

Select bibliography

For the select bibliography my choice of books has been determined by the relevance of the studies to the theme of this work rather than by their status as the most comprehensive or up-to-date analysis of a particular dramatist or period.

This is the first study of tragicomedy to include a comprehensive analysis of the genre from the sixteenth century to the present day. A detailed study of neo-classical tragicomedy will be found in M. T. Herrick's *Tragicomedy: Its Origin and Development in Italy, France and England* (Urbana, Ill., 1955). On twentieth-century developments the most useful study is J. L. Styan's *The Dark Comedy: The Development of Modern Comic Tragedy* (Cambridge, 1962). For the relationship of the genre to those of tragedy and comedy Cyrus Hoy's *The Hyacinth Room: An Investigation into the Nature of Comedy, Tragedy and Tragicomedy* (London, 1967) is highly recommended. George Steiner, in his challenging work *The Death of Tragedy* (London, 1961), analyses the inability of tragedy to reflect the problems of the contemporary world and Walter Kerr's *Tragedy and Comedy* (London, 1967) begs some interesting questions relevant to this study.

1 Introduction

The following editions are recommended: Sir Philip Sidney, *The Defence of Poesie* ed. J. A. van Dorsten (Oxford, 1966); John Dryden, *Of Dramatick Poesie* ed. J. T. Boulton (Oxford, 1964); Thomas Preston, *Cambises*, in *Tudor Plays* ed. E. Creeth (New York, 1966); John Fletcher, *The Faithful Shepherdess* ed. J. St Loe Strachey (Mermaid, London, 1893) – quotations are from the

Complete Works of Beaumont and Fletcher, ed. H. Weber (Edinburgh, 1812). G. Guarini's important essay *Compendio della Poesia Tragicomica* is not available in English; quotations are from the edition in the series *Scrittori d'Italia* ed. Gioachino Brognolio (Bari, 1914), the translations are mine.

Bernard F. Dukore's *Dramatic Theory and Criticism* (New York, 1974) is a comprehensive selection of extracts from major documents in dramatic theory, including Guarini's *Compendio*. Another useful study is *Aristotle's Theory of Poetry and Fine Art* ed. S. H. Butcher (London, 1951).

2   Seventeenth-century pastoral and tragicomedy

There are two editions of Richard Fanshawe's translation of Guarini's *Il Pastor Fido* (*The Faithful Shepherd*): ed. William E. Simeone and Walter Staton Jr (Oxford, 1964); ed. J. Whitfield (Edinburgh, 1976), with parallel Italian text. It is also included in Penguin's *Five Italian Renaissance Comedies* (Harmondsworth, 1978). Quotations from Shakespeare are from the *Complete Works* ed. Peter Alexander (London, 1951).

Una Ellis-Fermor's *The Jacobean Drama* (London, 1936), *Elizabethan Drama* ed. R. J. Kaufmann (New York, 1961) and *Stratford-upon-Avon Studies* I: *Jacobean Theatre* ed. J. R. Brown and B. Harris (London, 1960) all contain important chapters or essays. For a more detailed discussion of *The Tempest* in relation to the writings of Guarini see David L. Hirst's study in Macmillan's 'Text and Performance' series (London, 1984).

3   Comedy in tragedy: Elizabethan and Jacobean theatre

The following editions are recommended: Christopher Marlowe, *The Jew of Malta* ed. T. W. Craik (The New Mermaids, London, 1966); Christopher Marlowe, *Doctor Faustus* ed. J. D. Jump (The Revels Plays, London, 1962); John Marston, *The Malcontent* ed. M. L. Wine (Regents Renaissance Drama Series, London, 1965);

Thomas Middleton and William Rowley, *The Changeling* ed.
N. W. Bawcutt (The Revels Plays, London, 1966); Cyril Tour-
neur, *The Revenger's Tragedy* ed. R. A. Foakes (The Revels
Plays, London, 1966); John Webster, *The Duchess of Malfi* ed.
J. R. Brown (The Revels Plays, London, 1964); John Webster,
The White Devil ed. J. R. Brown (The Revels Plays, London,
1960).

T. S. Eliot's *Elizabethan Dramatists* (London, 1963) is a pioneer
and influential work, worthy of some detailed study. The books by
Ellis-Fermor, Kaufmann and Brown and Harris listed above contain material which is also relevant here. Section IV, by Alvin
Kernan, of *The Revels History of Drama in English, Vol. III* ed.
C. Leech and T. W. Craik (London, 1975) is a recent survey of
dramatic trends in the late sixteenth and early seventeenth centuries. F. Bowers's *Elizabethan Revenge Tragedy* (Princeton, NJ,
1940) remains the most thorough exploration of the complex ethical and dramatic issues of this important tragicomic genre.

4 French seventeenth-century tragicomedy

All quotations from Corneille and Racine are taken from the
Larousse editions. There is a particular problem of translation in
the case of Corneille. I have therefore quoted from *Le Cid* both in
the original and in the literal, but unpoetic Penguin edition, trans.
J. Cairncross (Harmondsworth, 1975).

Martin Turnell's *The Classical Moment* (London, 1947) provides a stimulating introduction to the literary and philosophical
background of the period. A useful short introduction to Corneille,
with analyses of the three plays discussed in this chapter, is J. H.
Broome's *A Student's Guide to Corneille* (London, 1971). The most
detailed study available in English is P. J. Yarrow's *Corneille*
(London, 1963). G. Pocock's *Corneille and Racine: Problems of
Tragic Form* (Cambridge, 1973) explores the wider implications of
dramatic structure discussed in this work.

5 Melodrama

The three major collections of nineteenth-century melodramas are: *Nineteenth-Century Plays* ed. G. Rowell (Oxford, revised 1972) which includes *Black-Ey'd Susan, The Colleen Bawn, Lady Audley's Secret* and *The Bells; The Magistrate and Other Nineteenth-Century Plays* ed. M. Booth (Oxford, 1974) which includes *The Factory Lad;* and *Victorian Melodramas* ed. J. L. Smith (London, 1976) which includes *The Drunkard.*

Jerome K. Jerome's *Stageland* (London, 1889) is a diverting and often accurate comment on the conventions as they relate to tragicomedy. Michael Booth's *English Melodrama* (London, 1965) is also recommended.

6 Variations of melodrama: Chekhov and Shaw

Quotations from Chekhov's plays are from the Penguin edition, trans. Elisaveta Fen (Harmondsworth, 1959), with the exception of *The Wood Demon* which will be found in the Everyman edition, trans. S. S. Koteliansky (London, 1937). Quotations from Shaw are from *The Works of Bernard Shaw* (London, 1931–50).

Robert Brustein's *The Theatre of Revolt* (London, 1965) contains some valuable essays on both Chekhov and Shaw. J. L. Styan's *Chekhov in Performance* (Cambridge, 1971) is an interesting theatrical study while Margery M. Morgan's *The Shavian Playground* (London, 1972) has a more literary emphasis. A useful chapter on melodrama can be found in Martin Meisel, *Shaw and the Nineteenth-Century Theatre* (Princeton, NJ, 1963).

7 Twentieth-century pioneers

Only two plays by Luigi Pirandello are available in English, *Henry IV* (London, 1979) and *Six Characters in Search of an Author* (London, 1979). Also available is his *L'Umorismo* (*On Humor*), trans. A. Illiano and D. P. Testa, *Studies in Comparative Literature,* 58

134   *Tragicomedy*

(Chapel Hill, NC, 1974). H. L. Bergson's *Laughter* is quoted from the translation by C. Brereton and F. Rothwell (London, 1913). Bertolt Brecht's *Messingkauf Dialogues* (London, 1965) and his plays are published by Methuen. Four volumes of Antonin Artaud's *Collected Works* are now available (London, 1968–74). Eugène Ionesco's comprehensive *Plays*, trans. D. Watson (London, 1958–80) is the best available source in English. Samuel Beckett's works are largely available from Faber and Calder & Boyars.

For Pirandello the relevant chapters in Robert Brustein's *The Theatre of Revolt* (London, 1965) are recommended as is Eric Bentley's *Theatre of War* (New York, 1954). A useful introductory study is S. Bassnett-McGuire, *Luigi Pirandello* (London, 1983). On Brecht, John Willett's *The Theatre of Bertolt Brecht* (London, 1959) provides a sound introduction although Jan Needle and Peter Thomson's *Brecht* (Oxford, 1981) is more stimulating. Martin Esslin's *Antonin Artaud* (London, 1976) is concise while *Artaud and After* by Ronald Hayman (Oxford, 1977) has a more theatrical emphasis. A great deal has been written on Absurd Theatre. Martin Esslin's *The Theatre of the Absurd* (Harmondsworth, revised 1968) was the pioneer study of the genre and remains the most comprehensive. A. P. Hinchliffe's *The Absurd* (London, 1969) is a useful short introduction. L. C. Pronko's *Avant Garde: The Experimental Theatre in France* (London, 1962) is a stimulating book, more concerned with tragicomic features. Detailed studies of two key dramatists are P. Murray, *The Tragic Comedian: A Study of Samuel Beckett* (Cork, 1970) and *Ionesco* ed. R. C. Lamont (Englewood Cliffs, NJ, 1973).

8   Old ways, new directions

Peter Nichols is published by Faber, Peter Barnes by Heinemann and Edward Bond by Methuen.

There is no detailed study of Peter Nichols. Bernard F. Dukore's *The Theatre of Peter Barnes* (London, 1981) is a detailed exploration of the theatrical extremes employed by this dramatist. The most comprehensive analysis of Edward Bond is *Bond: A Study of his Plays* by M. Hay and P. Roberts (London, 1980), although it is not concerned with his stature as a tragicomic dramatist. *Stratford-upon-Avon Studies* XIX: *Contemporary English Drama* ed. M. Bradbury and D. Palmer (London, 1981) is a cross-section of recent opinion on new trends in English theatre. Helpful background studies on modern drama are J. Elsom, *Post-War British Theatre* (London, 1976), A. P. Hinchliffe, *British Theatre 1950–1970* (Oxford, 1974), J. R. Taylor, *The Second Wave* (London, 1971) and K. J. Worth, *Revolutions in Modern English Drama* (London, 1973).

Index

138   *Tragicomedy*